Ethnic Needlepoint

Ethnic Needlepoint

DESIGNS FROM
ASIA, AFRICA AND THE AMERICAS

MARY NORDEN

PHOTOGRAPHS BY SIMON BROWN

WATSON-GUPTILL PUBLICATIONS

NEW YORK

First published in the
United States of America in 1993 by
Watson-Guptill Publications Inc.
1515 Broadway, New York NY 10036

Text and designs copyright ©
Mary Norden 1993
The moral right of the Author
has been asserted

Photographs copyright ©
George Weidenfeld & Nicolson Ltd
1993

First published in 1993 by
George Weidenfeld & Nicolson Ltd
Orion House
5 Upper St Martin's Lane
London WC2H 9EA

Libaray of Congress
Cataloguing-in-Publication Data
A catalogue record for this book
is available from the Library of
Congress.

ISBN 0-8230-1605-6

Designed by Roger Davies
Charts by Malcolm Couch
Illustrations by Sarah Davies
Set design by David Campbell
Styling by Mary Norden
Jacket photograph by Tim Imrie

Phototypeset by Keyspools Ltd,
Golborne, Lancs, UK
in Palatino
Colour separations by
Newsele Litho Ltd, UK
Printed in Italy by
Printers Srl, Trento
Bound by L.E.G.O., Vicenza

Contents

Acknowledgements

It has been a great pleasure and a wonderfully colourful experience writing this book, but it would never have been completed without the help and support of so many people.

For hours of stitching, grateful thanks to Joan Eve, Jane Harding, Rachael Kingman, Angela Knight, Jane Manley, Anne Newman, Elizabeth Norden, Pat Taylor and especially Phyllis Kingman, Ann Steer and Mary Stenning. For their enthusiastic support in finding more stitchers, thank you to Douglas and Mary Ann Garrad, and Shirley Jones. For coping with the typing so calmly and efficiently, thank you to Sheila Dunn and Jayne Wright of Martello Office Services. For his photograph on pages 68–9, Tim Imrie. Particular thanks for their enormous generosity in lending so many wonderful objects goes to Alison Bentz of South American Design, Davies, Gill Lloyd, Lesley Gilder, Jenny Hayward-Karlsson, Pip Rau and David Wainwright. For her continual encouragement and above all her optimism, my agent Frances Kelly. For her meticulous technical illustrations thank you to Sarah Davies. A special thank you to Simon Brown for his glorious photography, to David Campbell for his splendid and inspired sets and to Roger Davies, who managed to bring together through a maze of pictures, text and deadlines, such a magnificently designed book. And lastly, but most importantly, a very special thank you to Suzannah Gough, my editor, who carried me through the whole project with her constant support, terrifying efficiency, and above all, her sense of humour.

This book is dedicated to Charles

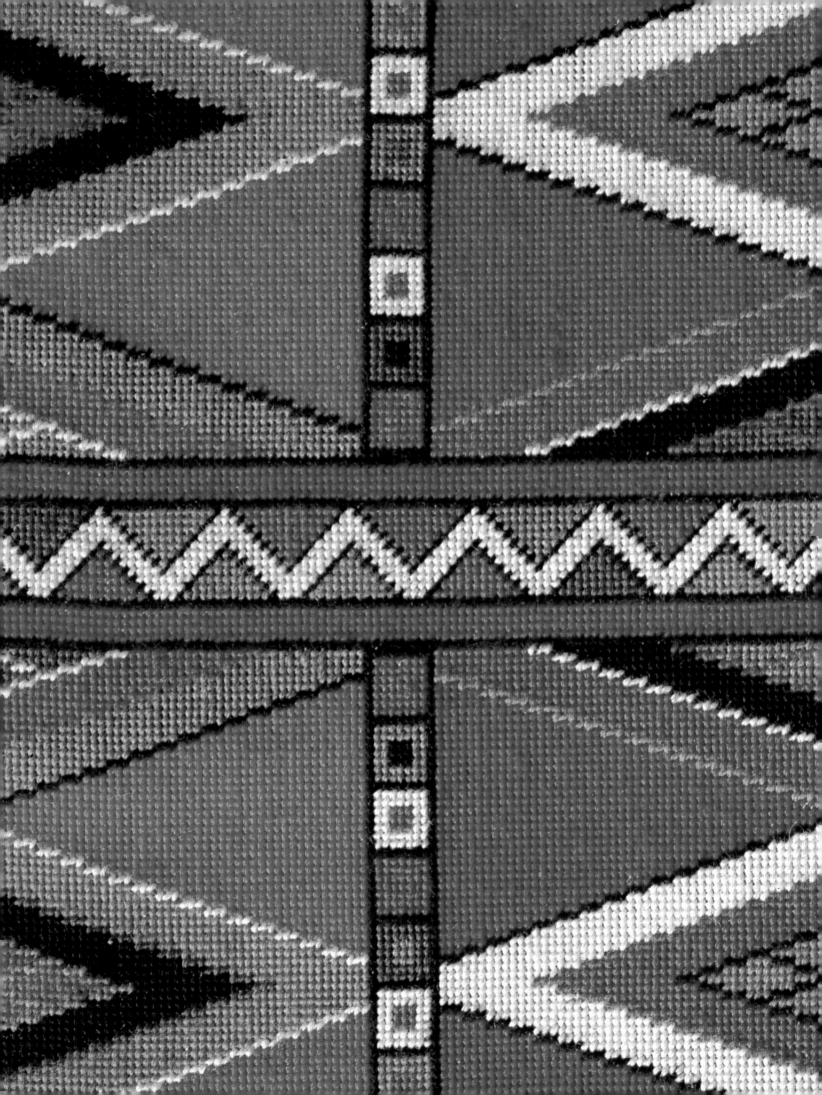

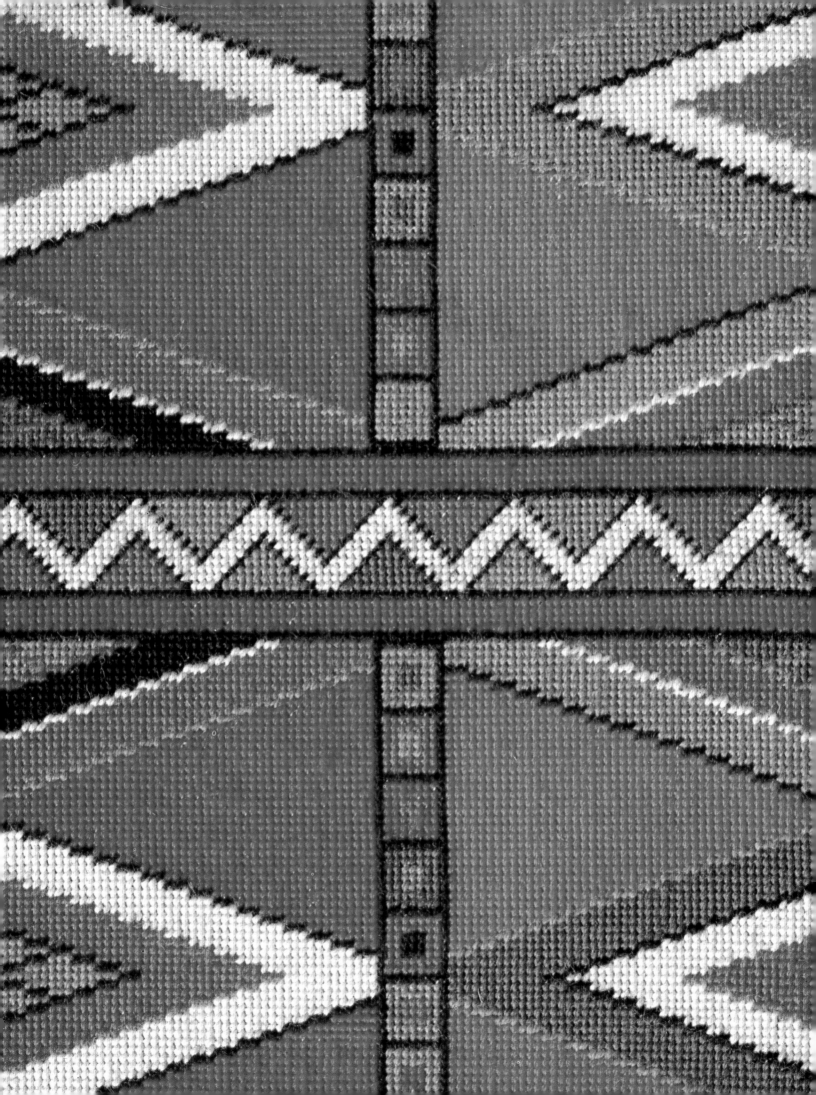

Introduction

This book celebrates the colour and pattern of ethnic art and translates it into designs for needlepointers who are looking for fresh ideas and challenges. I also hope that it will encourage less experienced needlepointers and stimulate a creative interest in each person so that they can go on to select their own colours and patterns.

My own fascination for colour began as a child when I had a weakness for coloured paper and at school collected boxes of crayons as avidly as a train spotter spots trains. Later, at college, when I was studying textiles, I mixed dyes on a grand scale. Wherever I go and whatever I see, it is always colour that I notice and remember first, whether it is colours mixed by nature, such as the passionate red of a rose, the sharp yellow of a lemon or the navy of a thunderous sky, or those mixed by man, such as the faded pinks of Venice, the shimmering blues of a Monet painting or the hard graphic greys of a newspaper. And with colour comes pattern in a multitude of styles. In addition to those found in nature there are those created by man from his constant urge to decorate, to adorn not just his house and furniture but also his textiles, ceramics, utensils

and even his own body. From this fusion of palette and design, it is the art of the tribespeople from all over the world, past and present, that I find the most stimulating and expressive. Again and again I return to ethnic culture, in particular the textiles, for inspiration. You cannot fail to notice the breathtaking diversity of ideas, or the labour-intensive craftsmanship that is worked into each and every piece. In this respect, ethnic art recalls a way of life that was once prevalent in pre-industrial Europe.

I have been lucky. In my many years as a textile designer living in London I have had numerous opportunities to explore the fruits of these tribespeople. I have been to many wonderful exhibitions and museums, had access to the riches of private collectors, the use of the vast Victoria and Albert art library and browsed in many ethnic specialist shops that now exist. I have also travelled, not on any grand eighteenth-century scale, but on several short trips to experience at first hand the cultures of some of these tribespeople. On these visits I take a sketch book and camera to record images, patterns and, most importantly for me, the colour. For however good photography might be, you will always lose some of the spirit of the local colour.

I wanted to exploit the rich source of imagery which I have gathered from these forays into ethnic art and what better way than by creating a collection of designs for needlepoint, a pastime I have enjoyed for many years and which today is experiencing a huge revival. However, the range of ethnic materials and designs is so enormous that I had to limit myself to something more manageable, so I decided to place the emphasis on 'tribal' textiles, ignoring all workshop production. I drew on the many styles of the woven kilim found throughout Asia, the vivid Berber rugs from Morocco, the vibrant woven fabrics of Guatemala and Mexico, the mysterious imagery of Peru and the intricate embroideries of an Indian girl's dowry, to mention just a few.

The art of translating pattern onto canvas for needlepoint is not difficult, even less so if one limits oneself to a few basic stitches. My personal priority has always been for colour and pattern, rather than creating texture by the use of various technical skills. The bold style of patterning frequently found in ethnic art lends itself almost effortlessly to the process of needlepoint and, particularly when arranged in a repeat, allows enormous scope for playing with different colours, something I wanted to stress in this book.

When I chose the colours for each design, I did not always confine myself to the original source of inspiration, but for many of the projects stitched the designs in two colourways; this was to illustrate how easily ethnic patterns adapt to a multitude of colour combinations, from sharp and bright to dark and subtle tones. I hope this book will encourage people not just to work with the colourways I have chosen but to create their own. It helps to remember when choosing and combining colours that strong vibrant tones, as used for example in Mexican Stars (pages 124–9), will be a dominant and colourful feature in a room, while the mellow mix of faded pinks, blues and browns used in a design like Nomadic Star (pages 60–63) will, by comparison, blend more easily with the decor of the room. Likewise with patterns: some designs, such as the Turkistan Eagle footstool (pages 42–5) will stand out in a room much more than the subtle patterning of a design like Eastern Flower (pages 26–31) which will be more discreet.

When I conceived the idea of this book, I wanted to convey a little about ethnic style, not just through the designs and the text, but also through the photography and the use of just a few ethnic objects. With very simple styling, each project was shot against a coloured background to emphasize the imaginative use of colour in tribal living – the turquoise of a Mexican home, the mud brown of an African hut or the mix of terracotta and plum in an Indian interior. I wanted each picture to be uncluttered to reflect the nineties lifestyle which we are moving towards. During the eighties, houses were furnished in either a grand country house style of chintz and swagged curtains, fat sofas and hundreds of ornaments, or in a hard minimal style of angular furniture, matt black and venetian blinds. As people have travelled further afield, leaving Europe in preference for more exotic holiday destinations, they have returned laden with ethnic objects from India, Africa and Mexico, each object appreciated for its individuality and not part of a Western mass-produced lifestyle. People have at last become aware of the splendour and great diversity of ethnic style.

In response to ethnic style establishing itself as the look of the nineties and with the lack of designs encapsulating the many exotic features of tribal textiles, I have created this collection of needlepoint designs. I hope you will feel the same excitement and stimulation when stitching them as I felt when creating this book and will be aroused to start your own journey through the wonderfully colourful world of ethnic culture.

Asia

I remember clearly the day my parents bought a Persian carpet which was then delivered to our house. It was unrolled to display a dazzling pattern of exquisite meanderings of vine leaves, carnations, roses and tulips, and the colours were those of a long summer which seemed to glow even in the dark. I soon learnt that this magical carpet came from a completely different culture to the one I knew, and its design was rich with mysterious symbolic meaning. So it was that at the age of eight I was introduced to the beautiful textiles of Asia.

Since then I've come to learn that over the centuries Asia has produced a great wealth of textiles, not just woven but embroidered, appliquéd, printed, and tie-dyed as well, and as varied in style as its landscape and its people. In addition to the sumptuous floral carpets of Persia, I have discovered, to mention only a few, the lively figurative patterns of the colourful village embroideries and appliqué work from the Indian states of Gujarat, Rajasthan and Punjab; the distinctive animal and bird motifs splendid with their heraldic appearance that adorn the animal covers and saddlebags of Azerbaijan; the intricate paisley patterns of the much sought after Kashmir shawl; the ikat – a dyeing technique wherein the yarn is resist dyed before weaving to create shimmering silk patterns of abstract forms – made into luxurious coats for the elite of Turkestan.

It is the wonderfully expressive weaving of the many different nomads wandering across Asia, and in particular the kilim, a flat woven rug, that I look to again and again for inspiration. The breathtaking diversity of colour and pattern found within these kilims has influenced much of my work, inspiring designs such as Eastern Flower, Afghan Patchwork and Nomadic Star, all of which appear in this book. From the eastern Mediterranean shoreline, where the cultures of Europe and Asia blend, come large, gloriously coloured kilims full of simple floral motifs clustered around a tree of life. Moving slowly east towards the mountains of Central Anatolia come a profusion of prayer rugs, well known for their yellow ochre colouring and representations of the prayer arch, the 'mihrab', surrounded by distinctive floral and leaf borders. Across the border into the original Soviet states of Azerbaijan, Armenia and Georgia, known collectively as the Caucasus, you will find two very different styles: large kilims patterned with very colourful and bold abstract medallions, all framed by a border, or the more common borderless rug, subtly patterned with stripes of smaller geometric shapes in softer harmonious colours. From Persia comes an abundance of rugs finely decorated with floral motifs arranged in many different and wonderful compositions. Travelling further east up onto the arid plains and frozen peaks of the barren mountains of Afghanistan, kilims become larger and more robust, sometimes woven in sombre colours with minimal pattern and others woven with the distinctive eight-legged spider motif in bright blues and reds. Bolder still are the geometrically patterned rugs of the gypsies from this region, with amazingly garish colours and elaborate fringe decorations of beads, shells and even coins. As with all Asian textiles, nomadic rugs show a rich profusion of colour that ranges from subtle earth tones to vibrant reds, blues, greens and yellows that dazzle together and thrill the eye.

It is important to remember that for over a thousand years the nomads have developed and woven these textiles not just for decoration but also for utility reasons. When they settle in their temporary encampments, the nomads use these multi-coloured textiles for warmth and shade as well as to create walls, ceilings, and even furniture within the interiors of their tents. The textiles also have a symbolic language developed according to the beliefs and religion of the people: the tree of life for example is one of the most potent symbols. It links the underworld to the earth and the earth to the heavens; the common eye motif, as well as the ram's horns and pairs of birds, is intended to protect against the evil onlooker; the abundance of floral motifs, particularly in the flat woven rug, reflects an appreciation for the flower in an often dry and dusty climate.

I only have the space to mention just a few of the many different styles to be found, not only amongst the glorious rugs, but in all forms of textiles. I hope you come to learn even a little about them during the course of this book and to feel as enthusiastic as I do.

CAUCASIAN MEDALLION

CAPTIVATED BY THE EXQUISITE CARPETS OF
THE CAUCASUS, THIS BOLD DESIGN ONLY
HINTS AT THE PARADISE OF GEOMETRIC
PATTERN WAITING TO ASTOUND YOU.

In the cold mountain regions of Azerbaijan, a state of the Caucasus and an area steeped in an atmosphere of domestic carpet weaving, girls from their earliest years would help their mothers to prepare and spin the wool, to dye it and then weave it into carpets, saddlebags and kilims, all richly patterned. Struck by the bold simplicity of the numerous geometric forms used, I chose just two motifs for this design, both commonly found in the borders of the Caucasian carpet; the medallion, for my central motif, and framing this, a row of shapes known as 'buttons'.

In addition to the endless design possibilities, these motifs offered inexhaustible scope for playing with colour. I worked Caucasian Medallion in just two colourways. For the first, seen in the cushion on the previous page, I chose colours that seem to sing together and for the second, as used for this director's chair, a more subtle combination. I extended the design to fit the chair simply by repeating the border pattern along two edges to obtain extra width. Very simple yet so wonderfully effective. If you are daunted by working both the seat and the back of the chair in needlepoint, just stitch one piece and upholster the other in a complementary fabric. Experiment with the motifs to create your own designs as well as your own colour combination.

Caucasian Medallion chart

MATERIALS

Yarn Appleton tapestry wool in the following colours and approximate amounts:

Cushion: colourway 1

	605	18 yd/16 m		696	29 yd/26 m
	155	53 yd/48 m		242	20 yd/18 m
	504	34 yd/31 m		588	42 yd/38 m
	226	34 yd/31 m		691	34 yd/31 m
	714	31 yd/28 m			

Chair: colourway 2

		Seat	Back
	186	30 yd/27 m	9 yd/8 m
	504	42 yd/38 m	28 yd/26 m
	714	26 yd/24 m	10 yd/9 m
	748	28 yd/26 m	12 yd/11 m
	645	20 yd/18 m	12 yd/11 m
	695	29 yd/26 m	33 yd/30 m
	765	33 yd/30 m	13 yd/12 m
	155	22 yd/20 m	8 yd/7 m
	691	77 yd/70 m	21 yd/19 m
	998	74 yd/67 m	31 yd/28 m

Canvas: 12-mesh single canvas:
Cushion: 19″/49 cm square.
Chair seat: 23″/58 cm × 19″/49 cm.
Chair back: 23″/58 cm × 11″/28 cm.

Finishing materials: Cushion: ½ yd/50 cm of backing fabric and matching thread.
12″/30 cm zip fastener. 62″/157 cm of cord for edging (optional).
Chair seat: ½ yd/50 cm of backing fabric and matching thread.
Chair back: ¼ yd/30 cm of backing fabric and matching thread.

Charted design area
Cushion: 181 stitches wide by 181 stitches high.
Chair seat: 219 stitches wide by 181 stitches high.
Chair back: 219 stitches wide by 85 stitches high.

Finished design
Cushion: 15″/38 cm square.
Chair seat: 18¼″/46 cm × 15″/38 cm.
Chair back: 18¼″/46 cm × 7″/17.5 cm.

ORDER OF WORK

Cushion For full practical information on methods used in order of work, refer to Needlepoint Techniques (pages 150–54). Prepare the canvas. The entire design is worked in half-cross stitch using 1 strand of yarn throughout. Each square on the chart represents one stitch on the canvas. Following the chart, complete the design, working in either colourway 1, as given with the chart, or in colourway 2, by referring to the photograph of the chair. Stretch the finished needlepoint before backing. Sew on cord if required.

Chair

Seat Following order of work as given for the cushion, complete the design, omitting at this stage the outer border of the triangles (a depth of 5 stitches). To add the extra width needed for the chair seat, repeat the 19 stitches of the floral border once more on both sides, before completing seat with an outer border of triangles.

Back Following the order of work as given for the cushion, first work 1 row of medallions, across centre of canvas with only 1 row of stitches in background colour above and below these motifs. Work inner border of triangles before working floral border, as for seat, adding extra width in the same way. Work outer border of triangles at sides only. Stretch both the finished seat and back before backing and assembling on chair.

EASTERN FLOWER

TO SEE THE BEAUTIFUL COLOUR COMBINATIONS AND DISTINCTIVE FLORAL AND GEOMETRIC DESIGNS OF THE KILIM RUG WHICH ARE EXPRESSED IN THIS CUSHION IS LIKE A JOURNEY OF UNENDING INSPIRATION.

The kilim, or flat-woven rug, was once known as the poor man's carpet. Woven mainly in wool and patterned with symbolic and tribal motifs, they were originally a means of exchange – especially as part of a dowry – as well as objects for domestic use. Kilims differed from region to region depending on the cultural influences. In my design the profusion of stylized flowers arranged in diagonal stripes of contrasting colours is typical. I have framed the central area, or field, as it is called, with a double border of stars and more flower heads. The rich and harmonious colours of the first colourway and the bright, lighter hues of the second, on the following page, are also typical of the kilim rug.

Eastern Flower

MATERIALS

Yarn Appleton tapestry wool in the following colours and approximate amounts:

Cushion: colourway 1

■	852	68 yd/62m
■	566	35 yd/32m
■	226	95 yd/87m
■	145	11 yd/10m
■	695	29 yd/26m
■	691	52 yd/47m

Cushion: colourway 2

■	691	34 yd/31m
■	186	22 yd/20m
■	714	25 yd/23m
■	504	38 yd/35m
■	566	50 yd/46m
■	695	25 yd/23m
■	242	23 yd/21m
■	565	15 yd/14m

Canvas: 12-mesh single canvas 19"/48 cm square.

Finishing materials: $\frac{1}{2}$ yd/50 cm of backing fabric and matching thread. 12"/30 cm zip fastener 62"/157 cm of cord for edging (optional).

Charted design area
180 stitches wide by 179 stitches high.

Finished design
15"/38 cm square.

ORDER OF WORK

For full practical information on methods used in order of work, refer to Needlepoint Techniques (pages 150–54). Prepare the canvas. The entire design is worked in half-cross stitch using 1 strand of yarn throughout. Each square on the chart represents one stitch on the canvas. Following the chart, complete the design, working in either colourway 1, as given with the chart, or in colourway 2, by referring to the photograph. Stretch the finished needlepoint before backing. Sew on cord if required.

AFGHAN PATCHWORK

QUIET AND RESTRAINED, BOLD AND BRILLIANT, COLOUR IS PART OF THE MAGIC OF ASIA. FROM ITS GLORIOUS PALETTE I CHOSE COLOURS REMINISCENT OF THE SUBTLE AND HARMONIOUS TONES OBTAINED FROM NATURAL DYES.

Before the first chemical dyes were introduced in the 1850s, dye could only be extracted from natural sources. The root of the madder plant or the cochineal worm gave red; the saffron crocus gave yellow, as did the skins of pomegranates and onions; the indigo plant gave blue; nutshells and bark from oak and walnut gave shades of brown; and ripe turmeric berries and yellow yarn with indigo gave green. There were differences in the colouring of the weaving as the same plants could not be found everywhere and also because different methods of dyeing were used from region to region. The recipes for these glorious colours that mellow so gently were handed down through generations by word of mouth, but many have now been lost forever.

Colour from natural dyes was indeed the inspiration for my Afghan Patchwork. Although I have used synthetic dyes I have tried to match the colours as closely as possible and for the predominantly red colourway, and its blue alternative, to use those colours that were most readily available to the nomadic tribes of Asia. The navy I have chosen through to the palest blue represents indigo; red and pink are madder; yellow is saffron; green is yellow yarn with indigo, and cream and dark brown are the natural colours of sheep's wool. This simple design lends itself to endless colourways, so dip into your own paintbox and mix combinations with as few as three colours or as many as twenty.

Afghan Patchwork chart

MATERIALS

Yarn Appleton tapestry wool in the following colours and approximate amounts.

Colourway 1

■	584	20 yd/18m
■	226	42 yd/38m
■	126	35 yd/32m
■	124	14 yd/13m
■	695	12 yd/11m
■	333	28 yd/26m
■	963	10 yd/9m
■	984	28 yd/26m

Colourway 2

■	852	65 yd/59m
■	853	46 yd/42m
■	566	44 yd/40m
■	226	28 yd/26m
■	124	28 yd/26m
■	922	25 yd/23m
■	984	28 yd/26m

Canvas: 13-mesh single canvas 18"/46cm square.

Finishing materials: ½ yd/50 cm of backing fabric and matching thread. 12"/30 cm zip fastener. 60"/152 cm of cord for edging (optional).

Charted design area
191 stiches wide by 191 stitches high

Finished design
14½"/37 cm square.

ORDER OF WORK

Rug For full practical information on methods used in order of work refer to Needlepoint Techniques (pages 150–54). Prepare the canvas. The size of a finished piece of needlepoint will depend not only on the chart size but also on the mesh size of the canvas used. By using 7-mesh (rather than 13-mesh single canvas as for the cushion below), and using 2 strands of yarn rather than one, the size of the finished piece can be increased from 15"/38 cm square to 27"/68.5 cm square. To calculate the amount of yarn you will need, select your colourway and then multiply the quantities given on the left two and a half times for each colour. A single piece this size would make a wonderful floor cushion. Alternatively, work two pieces as I have done and join them together to make a rug. How many pieces you make depends on how large you wish the rug to be, but don't forget to allow an additional 2"/5 cm margin of canvas around each design.

The entire design is worked in half-cross stitch using 2 strands throughout. Each square on the chart represents one stitch on the canvas. Following the chart, complete the design working to the photograph of the rug for colourway 1, or in colourway 2 as given with the chart. Stretch each finished needlepoint before joining carefully (see page 152) and backing.

Cushion Follow order of work as given for the rug but use only 1 strand of yarn throughout. Stretch the finished needlepoint before backing. Sew on cord if required.

INDIAN BAZAAR

INSPIRED BY THE BEAUTIFUL EMBROIDERIES THAT EMBELLISH THE GIFTS OF THE INDIAN BRIDE, THESE THREE SPECTACLE CASES ONLY HINT AT THE RANGE AND PROFUSION OF EXOTIC DESIGN AND COLOUR SO TYPICAL OF INDIAN CULTURE.

An Indian girl with the women of her family will spend much of her childhood working richly embroidered textiles for her dowry. To her new home, the bride will bring costumes both for herself and the groom, hangings to furnish and decorate the house with and trappings for the domestic animals — all richly patterned with intricate embroidery or appliqué work and often incorporating small mirrors. These distinctive designs are abstract or very formalized representations of flowers, foliage, birds, animals and local mythology and are worked as colourfully as possible. The display of embroidery is of great importance at wedding celebrations and in addition to her dowry the bride will bring embroidered gifts – purses and bags – to be exchanged as part of the marriage ritual.

Immersed in the abundance of Indian embroidery and thinking of the wedding gifts, I designed these three spectacle cases. For the first, I chose a colourful floral pattern derived from a wedding canopy; for the second a formalized peacock, the most popular bird motif used in Indian crafts; and for the third a geometric design typical of the wandering Banjara tribe. Spectacle cases make ideal presents and are quick and easy to do.

Indian Bazaar charts

MATERIALS

Yarn Appleton tapestry wool in the following colours and approximate amounts:

Spectacle Case 1

■	105	11 yd/10 m
■	504	13 yd/12 m
■	802	5 yd/5 m
■	242	6 yd/5 m
■	476	3 yd/3 m
■	474	2 yd/2 m
■	882	25 yd/23 m

Spectacle Case 2

■	504	9 yd/8 m
■	802	6 yd/5 m
■	894	7 yd/6 m
■	242	36 yd/33 m
■	475	6 yd/5 m
■	882	8 yd/7 m

Spectacle Case 3

■	998	16 yd/15 m
■	722	18 yd/16 m
■	225	16 yd/15 m
■	474	22 yd/20 m
■	242	5 yd/5 m
■	882	8 yd/7 m

Canvas: For each case, 13-mesh single canvas 9½"/24 cm square.

Finishing materials: Small amount of lining fabric and matching thread.

Charted design area

Spectacle Case 1: 96 stitches wide by 91 stitches high
Spectacle Case 2: 96 stitches wide by 94 stitches high
Spectacle Case 3: 96 stitches wide by 94 stitches high

Finished design

Spectacle Case 1: 8"/20 cm × 7½"/19 cm
Spectacle Case 2: 8"/20 cm × 8"/20 cm
Spectacle Case 3: 8"/20 cm × 8"/20 cm

ORDER OF WORK

(Order of work is the same for all three spectacle cases.) For full practical information on methods used in order of work, refer to Needlepoint Techniques (pages 150–54). Prepare the canvas. The entire design is worked in half-cross stitch using 1 strand of yarn throughout. Each square on the chart represents one stitch on the canvas. Following the chart, work each chart twice to stitch both sides of the case. Stretch the finished needlepoint before trimming the excess canvas to ½"/1 cm. Fold hem to wrong side along top and bottom edges. Cut lining the same size as the needlepoint adding ½"/1 cm seam allowance. Fold seam allowance to wrong side, press and pin to needlepoint. Stitch neatly to needlepoint. Fold needlepoint in half lengthways with wrong sides together and join seams using half-cross stitch.

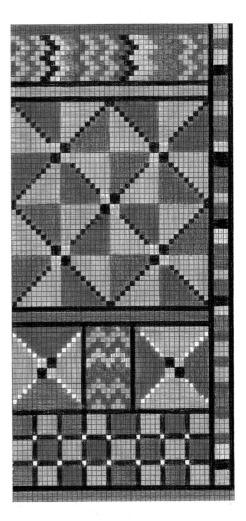

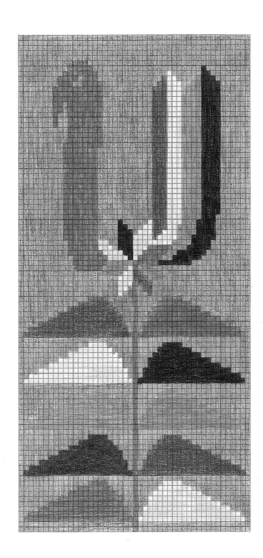

TURKESTAN EAGLE

AN ABSTRACT EAGLE WITH A JEWEL-LIKE BRILLIANCE ADORNS THIS FOOTSTOOL – A STYLE TYPICAL OF THE GLORIOUS PATTERNS FROM TURKESTAN THAT STRIKE OUT AGAINST A HARSH LANDSCAPE.

The fiercely independent nomadic herdsmen of the great steppes, desert and mountains of Turkestan live in large circular felt-covered tents. In the dark interior of these 'yurts' is a vibrant mix of colour and texture adorning every surface. Large patchwork panels of silk weaving, worked as dowry pieces, decorate the rear walls. Instead of wardrobes and shelves there are flatwoven and embroidered bags filled with utensils, clothing and cooking apparatus, and on the floor piles of colourful bedding, as well as rugs and carpets. It is not only the furnishings that add colour however but also the rich texture and patterning of the silk and cotton coats, the turbans and the dresses.

Taking a single motif from an embroidered breadbasket cover and enlarging it, I designed this striking footstool cover. It represents the double-headed eagle – an ancient Central Asian symbol of sovereignty. In Turkestan textiles, birds and animals are abstracted to the point of being unrecognizable.

If you prefer, you could simply use this design as a cushion. Be bold and work several pieces to make a vibrant group of cushions for your sofa or sew four pieces together for a wonderful floor cushion as described in the Needlepoint Techniques (pages 150–54).

Turkestan Eagle chart

MATERIALS

Yarn Appleton tapestry wool in the following colours and approximate amounts.

Footstool

■	998	4 yd/4 m
■	146	31 yd/28 m
▨	504	23 yd/21 m
■	105	16 yd/15 m
▨	313	32 yd/29 m
▨	475	17 yd/16 m
▨	691	5 yd/5 m

Canvas: 12-mesh single canvas 16″/41 cm square.

Finishing materials: 50″/127 cm of braid.

Charted design area
147 stiches wide by 147 stitches high.

Finished design
$12\frac{1}{4}$″/31 cm square.

ORDER OF WORK

For full information on methods used in order of work, refer to Needlepoint Techniques (pages 150–54). Prepare the canvas. The entire design is worked in half-cross stitch using 1 strand of yarn throughout. Each square on the chart represents one stitch on the canvas. Following the chart, complete the design. Stretch the finished needlepoint. Tack down the edges, pulling the needlepoint tight across the stool and positioning upholstery tacks as near as possible to the edges of the design. Cut excess canvas. Either stitch or paste on braid.

PERSIAN GARDEN

THE PERSIAN HAS ALWAYS BEEN A GREAT LOVER OF FLOWERS. SOME SAY THAT BY INTRODUCING THEM INTO HIS CARPET, HE FEELS THAT EVEN WHEN INSIDE HIS HOUSE OR DURING THE WINTER MONTHS HE IS SITTING IN HIS GARDEN.

From this desire to be in his garden at all times, the Persian gives us some of the finest floral carpets, abundant with pattern and intricate detail, typical of Persian art in all its forms, not just in its carpets but in its calligraphy, in the patterned tiles of its architecture and in its miniatures. From this daunting wealth of design I particularly wanted to use the 'boteh' motif, said to be the father of the paisley design. It resembles a leaf or a seed with its tip bent sideways and is highly stylized. It appears in endless variations, sometimes elaborate, sometimes simple, and not just in the Persian carpet but in those from the Caucasus as well.

For Persian Garden I chose two very different colourways. For the first, seen in this cushion, the dark sombre colours were inspired by an exhibition of textiles from Bhutan, a country where textiles are considered by its people to be the highest form of artistic expression.

In contrast to the first colourway, the colourway for this bolster is an abundance of bright, lighter hues – gold, orange, pink, green, blue and a lavish use of cream and navy for contrast. Instead of placing the motif on coloured vertical stripes, as I have done, you could try diagonal or horizontal stripes, even blocks of colour to create a patchwork effect, or for a far simpler pattern, work all the botehs on a single coloured background. I have used the same flowers to fill each boteh, but why not make every one different, not just filling it with flowers, but with leaves, animals, birds, figures or even gardening tools, anything you might find in your garden.

Persian Garden chart

MATERIALS

Yarn Appleton tapestry wool in the following colours and approximate amounts:

Cushion: colourway 1

■	998	83 yd/76m
■	504	119 yd/108m
■	696	60 yd/55m
■	345	70 yd/64m
■	964	37 yd/34m

Bolster: colourway 2

■	882	64 yd/58m
■	748	77 yd/70m
■	565	48 yd/44m
■	344	14 yd/13m
■	225	53 yd/48m
■	866	50 yd/46m
■	722	15 yd/14m
■	695	43 yd/39m

Canvas: For both cushion and bolster 12-mesh single canvas 21"/53 cm × 23"/59 cm.
Finishing materials: Cushion: $\frac{3}{4}$ yd/60 cm of backing fabric and matching thread. 14"/35 cm zip fastener. 74"/94 cm of cord for edging (optional). Bolster: $\frac{1}{4}$ yd/30 cm of fabric for bolster ends and matching thread. 2 button moulds. 2 tassels (optional).

Charted design area
200 stitches wide by 232 stitches high.

Finished design
17"/43 cm × 19$\frac{1}{4}$"/49 cm.

ORDER OF WORK

For full practical information on methods used in order of work refer to Needlepoint Techniques (pages 150–54). Prepare the canvas. The entire design is worked in half-cross stitch using 1 strand of yarn throughout. Each square on the chart represents one stitch on the canvas. Following the chart, work rows 1–116 and then repeat once more to complete the design. Work in either colourway 1, by referring to the photograph, or in colourway 2, as given with the chart. Stretch the finished needlepoint before either backing as for a cushion or making into a bolster (see page 153).

RAJASTHANI ELEPHANT

ACROSS A LAND OF PULSATING COLOUR,
WHERE EVERYTHING IS ADORNED TO
GLORIOUS EXCESS, THE MAJESTIC ELEPHANT
HAS BEEN USED FOR CENTURIES TO
DECORATE A RICH VARIETY OF TEXTILES.

When I designed Rajasthani Elephant, I wanted to portray some of the boldness of the appliqué designs from the villages of Western India that have influenced me. The large appliqués are usually used as canopies and friezes for celebrations or as animal trappings such as ox-covers, and are made with pieces of coloured fabric stitched onto a plain cotton ground. The designs are highly stylized and often pictorial, incorporating birds, animals and figures and their glorious colours — red, yellow, green, turquoise, pink, purple and shades of blue — bring relief to an arid landscape. The elephant in particular is often found in Indian appliqué and is held in high esteem as a powerful animal used for carrying a deity or king during important ceremonies.

To imitate the simplicity of these appliqués I used a coarser canvas, though the design would work equally well on a finer one, but add more elephants if you wish to keep the size of the original cushion. This is a wonderfully simple pattern with endless possibilities for using the elephant motif — for borders, chair and footstool covers, bolsters, spectacle cases, even belts. Abandon yourself to the vibrant colours and replace navy with cream, just one of the many colour options.

Rajasthani Elephant chart

MATERIALS

Yarn Appleton tapestry wool in the following colours and approximate amounts.

Cushion

■	852	135 yd/123 m
■	805	43 yd/39 m
■	823	9 yd/8 m
■	475	42 yd/38 m
■	994	8 yd/7 m
■	504	41 yd/37 m
■	947	28 yd/26 m
■	525	7 yd/6 m
■	894	10 yd/9 m
■	242	10 yd/9 m

Canvas: 7-mesh single thread canvas 23"/58 cm × 21"/53 cm.
Finishing materials: $\frac{3}{4}$ yd/60 cm of backing fabric and matching thread. 14"/35 cm zip fastener. 73"/185 cm of cord for edging (optional).

Charted design area
131 stitches wide by 119 stitches high.

Finished design
$18\frac{1}{2}$/4 cm × 17"/43 cm.

ORDER OF WORK

For full practical information on methods used in order of work, refer to Needlepoint Techniques (pages 150–54). Prepare the canvas. The entire design is worked in half-cross stitch using 2 strands of yarn throughout. Each square on the chart represents one stitch on the canvas. Following the chart, complete the design. Stretch the finished needlepoint before backing. Sew on cord if required.

NOMADIC STAR

THREE SIMPLE MOTIFS: A LEAF, A STAR AND A DIAMOND WORKED INTO A GLORIOUS KALEIDOSCOPE OF COLOUR AND PATTERN.

When the nomads began to introduce designs into their rugs they turned for inspiration to the natural objects that surrounded them – flowers, trees, animals, what they could see in the sky and the objects furnishing their tents. Simplified designs of these objects became more and more stylized, sometimes being transformed into merely abstract patterns.

For this design I took from the sky the eight pointed star – an ancient carpet ornament – and chose a diamond to contain it, and then placed both the motifs within a lattice of serrated leaves. I decorated this jewel-like pattern with a border of flowers and then mixed a palette of beautiful mellow colours.

Nomadic Star chart

MATERIALS

Yarn Appleton tapestry wool in the following colours and approximate amounts:

Cushion

■	588	60 yd/55 m
	691	29 yd/26 m
	696	56 yd/51 m
	226	20 yd/18 m
	504	17 yd/16 m
	714	26 yd/24 m
	225	26 yd/24 m
	722	12 yd/11 m
■	853	30 yd/27 m
	243	12 yd/11 m
	155	22 yd/20 m

Canvas: 12-mesh single canvas 19″/48 cm square.

Finishing materials: $\frac{1}{2}$ yd/50 cm of backing fabric and matching thread. 12″/30 cm zip fastener 62″/157 cm of cord for edging (optional).

Charted design area
179 stitches by 177 stitches high.

Finished design
15″/38 cm × 14$\frac{1}{2}$″/37 cm.

ORDER OF WORK

For full practical information on methods used in order of work, refer to Needlepoint Techniques (pages 150–54). Prepare the canvas. The entire design is worked in half-cross stitch using 1 strand of yarn throughout. Each square on the chart represents one stitch on the canvas. Following the chart, complete the design. Stretch the finished needlepoint before backing. Sew on cord if required.

Africa

As a child, the continent of Africa seemed to me an untamed land divided by the desert and scrub land of the Sahara. On one side, towards the Orient, there were the pyramids of Egypt and on the other side, Ingrid Bergman and Humphrey Bogart in the film *Casablanca* – both sides linked by a long and arduous camel journey which was made in stifling heat (I somehow thought this to be romantic) and which, with my brother and sister and the aid of a dressing up box, I tried to act out round the kitchen table.

After the start of geography lessons at school, Africa lost its romantic appeal and became instead a series of endless maps that quoted rainfall, river sources, population and trade. I learnt that it is a land of terrible disasters, where people have to contend with widely differing climates and landscapes, ranging from rain forests, through savannah, to arid expanses of desert. But no-one mentioned any of the visual elements of African culture. I first became aware of these quite by chance. A college tutor suggested that a visit to the library at the Museum of Mankind in London might help my essay on Eskimos. I spent a day there but never made it to the library.

Instead I discovered African art.

I saw carved ivory pendants and bracelets, masks, wooden combs, painted doors all richly patterned with symbolic and simple geometric motifs and representations of human beings, animals and mythical figures. Thus began an abiding fascination with a land full of objects of great primitive strength, beauty and style, and often of extraordinary craftsmanship. As I began to explore this wealth of art, I found that throughout the vastness of the continent the objects and their patterning changed according to the lifestyle and the cultural contacts of its people. They even changed within the terrain in which the tribes lived, differing from desert to forest and from savannah to mountainside. Materials, designs and techniques might be of local origin or brought along old trade routes; pieces might be inspired by local legends or beliefs, or simply by the creativity of a local craftsman. But nothing was merely decorative. Objects were carved, textiles patterned, jewellery crafted and bodies painted or decorated to express values, beliefs and achievements; they played roles in ritual and ceremony and they acted as safeguards against evil and diseases; in short, they served as a means of communication with their gods and ancestors.

In this chapter, I have chosen to focus on the textiles of Africa, starting in Tunisia, a short sea crossing from southern Europe. Here I found an abundance of woven rugs, intricately patterned in a mix of floral, figurative and geometric motifs worked in clear blues and yellows. Moving west into the often inhospitable slopes of the Atlas mountains of northern Africa, I sought out the glorious rugs of the numerous and flamboyant Berber tribes, appreciated for their luscious colour combinations and strong geometric styles. Moving south through the bush, scrub and grass plains to the equatorial forests of West Africa, I found a rich tradition of textiles. From Nigeria, plain or simply striped robes embellished at the neck with embroidered spirals, triangles, squares and circles. I also discovered fabrics decorated with an imaginative use of resist-dyeing techniques. Dye can be resisted by tye-dyeing or, for a more precise pattern, by sewing or tying sticks, stones or seeds into the fabric before dyeing it. From the tribes of Ghana comes cloth patterned with bands of different colours and designs. These strip-weavers are some of the most gloriously vibrant and highly patterned of African textiles and have influenced much of my work, inspiring in particular Scissors and Ladies (pages 72–9). Also from Ghana come the appliquéd and embroidered flags of the Asafo warriors, colourful with their childlike, decorative or abstract images. And finally, I was drawn to the geometric patterns of the Shoowa tribe of Zaire, who weave cloth with raffia and decorate it with sophisticated maze-like patterns full of interconnecting lines and squares in bold earthy colours.

And so I could continue travelling across what was once known as the 'Dark Continent', striving to capture in my work the powerful graphic patterns or the wonderful imagery which are duplicated free-hand in moments of self-expression over not just textiles but also wood carvings, jewellery, utensils and even the body. I do urge you to go to your local museum and discover for yourself the art of Africa and absorb the wealth of colour and pattern. In addition, read the numerous books now available and seek out the many specialist shops and galleries that have opened to meet the demand created by the new awareness of ethnic style.

ZULU CHEVRON

DECORATE YOUR HOME WITH A LITTLE OF
THE MAGIC OF AFRICA – DANCING
CHEVRONS, SIMPLE STRIPES AND DIAMONDS
COMBINED WITH THE COLOURS OF THE
EARTH.

Pursuing my love of geometric patterns, I was
drawn immediately to the painted houses and
village walls of southern Africa. Women use
basic tools or just their fingers to cover every
surface of their home, vigorously working in a
patchwork of abstract shapes, squares, triangles,
chevrons and rectangles. These are painted in an
endless range of subtle earth colours and often
sharply outlined in black. Pigment for painting is
obtained from clay, river mud, cow-dung and
juices from a variety of berries and plants.

Working with these same colours and thinking
of the painted houses, I wanted to apply
needlepoint in a different way, as though I too
were decorating walls rather than fabric. Most
designs for needlepoint are worked to a square
format and when complete become cushions. A
lampshade seemed ideal for the bold simplicity
of this pattern. I chose two rows of triangles,
coloured them randomly and below this added a
large chevron to dance round the light.

Zulu Chevron chart

MATERIALS

Yarn   Appleton tapestry wool in the following colours and approximate amounts.

Lampshade

▪	588	39 yd/36 m
	761	25 yd/23 m
▫	695	15 yd/14 m
▪	765	30 yd/27 m
▪	722	29 yd/26 m
▪	714	10 yd/9 m

Canvas: 12-mesh interlocked canvas 21″/53 cm × 14″/35 cm.

Finishing materials: Lampshade frame 8″/20 cm diameter × 5″/13 cm high. 38″/97 cm of cord for edging (optional). Lining paper.

Charted design area
201 stitches wide by 100 stitches high.

Finished design
17″/43 cm × 8″/20 cm.

ORDER OF WORK

For full practical information on methods used in order of work, refer to Needlepoint Techniques (pages 150–54). Prepare the canvas. The entire design is worked in half-cross stitch using 1 strand of yarn throughout. Each square on the chart represents one stitch on the canvas. Following the chart, complete the design. Stitch the finished needlepoint. Trim the excess canvas. Join the two straight edges using small backstitches and then sew to frame. Line the shade with paper and trim top and bottom with cord if required.

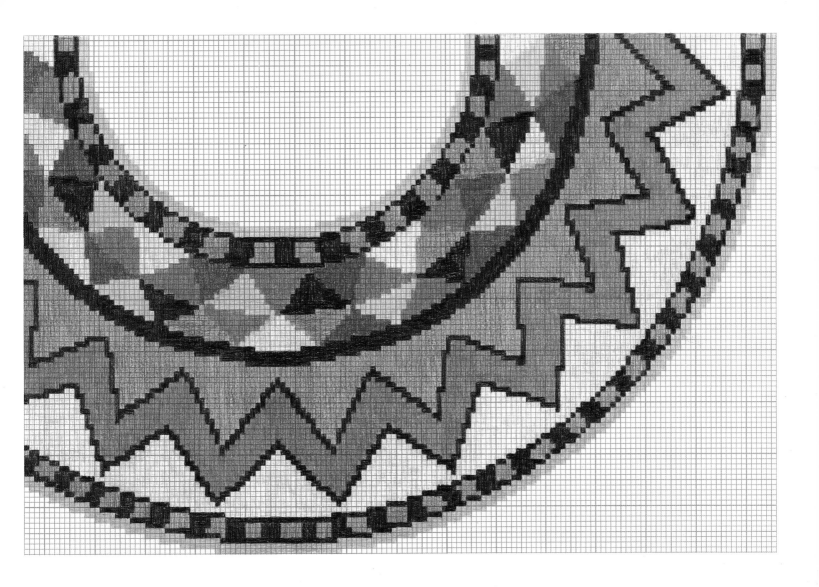

SCISSORS AND LADIES

STRUCK BY THE BOLD
IMAGES FOUND IN WEST
AFRICAN WEAVING, I
WANTED TO CREATE A
DESIGN USING MOTIFS THAT
WOULD REMIND ME OF ALL
THE WONDERFUL LADIES
WHO HAVE HELPED TO
STITCH THE DESIGNS FOR
THIS BOOK.

From the heat and dampness of the tropics of West Africa come the dazzling strip weaves of the Ashanti and Ewe tribes. Cloth is patterned with bands of different colours and designs, which create a colourful chequerboard effect. These bands, each three to ten inches wide, are woven in cotton and silk using a small portable loom. They are then cut and sewn together lengthways to make up toga-like wraps for men and women as well as cloth for blankets and wall hangings. The weaver may join up to one hundred of these narrow bands and will require great skill and experience to match the pattern from one strip to another. Colour is used with great verve, ranging from numerous blue and white combinations to the acid bright colours of lime green, yellow, vivid blue and shocking pink, which produce frenzied clashes. The woven motifs which dramatically adorn the cloth are either simple geometric shapes such as diamonds, crosses or stars, or naturalistic images from everyday life, such as fish, birds, people, utensils and even cars and aeroplanes.

For this design, dedicated to all my needlepoint ladies, I chose figures, hands and pairs of scissors and arranged them in blocks. It is not just this arrangement of pattern but also the two colourways I chose for this design that are typical of West African strip weaving.

For the first colourway (on the previous page) hot earth tones and olive green are dramatically set off against navy and for the second colourway, in complete contrast to the first, I chose the classic cool combination of different shades of blue with cream and a hint of terracotta. Don't restrict yourself to these two colourways, create your own. It is a wonderful design for using up odd bits of yarn. Design your own motifs, which could perhaps tell a story, or use letters and numbers to celebrate and record a birth or marriage. The possibilities are endless.

Scissors and Ladies chart

MATERIALS

Yarn   Appleton tapestry wool in the following colours and approximate amounts:

Cushion: colourway 1

■	928	69 yd/63 m
□	882	15 yd/14 m
▨	152	35 yd/32 m
▢	694	13 yd/12 m
▨	311	21 yd/19 m
▨	994	20 yd/18 m
▨	504	14 yd/13 m
■	948	21 yd/19 m
▨	242	13 yd/12 m

Cushion: colourway 2

■	852	13 yd/12 m
□	882	61 yd/56 m
■	853	52 yd/47 m
▨	568	28 yd/26 m
▨	565	18 yd/16 m
▨	922	17 yd/16 m
▨	722	13 yd/12 m

Canvas: 12-mesh single canvas 18″/46 cm square.

Finishing materials: ½ yd/50 cm of backing fabric and matching thread. 12″/30 cm zip fastener. 60″/152 cm of cord for edging (optional).

Charted design area
175 stitches wide by 175 stitches high.

Finished design
14½″/37 cm square.

ORDER OF WORK

For full practical information on methods used in order of work, refer to Needlepoint Techniques (pages 150–54). Prepare the canvas. The entire design is worked in half-cross stitch using 1 strand of yarn throughout. Each square on the chart represents one stitch on the canvas. Following the chart, complete the design, working in either colourway 1, as given with the chart, or in colourway 2, by referring to the photograph. Stretch the finished needlepoint before backing. Sew on cord if required.

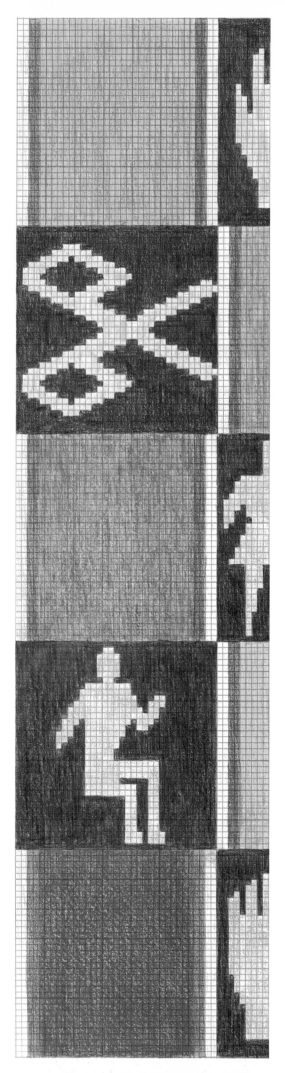

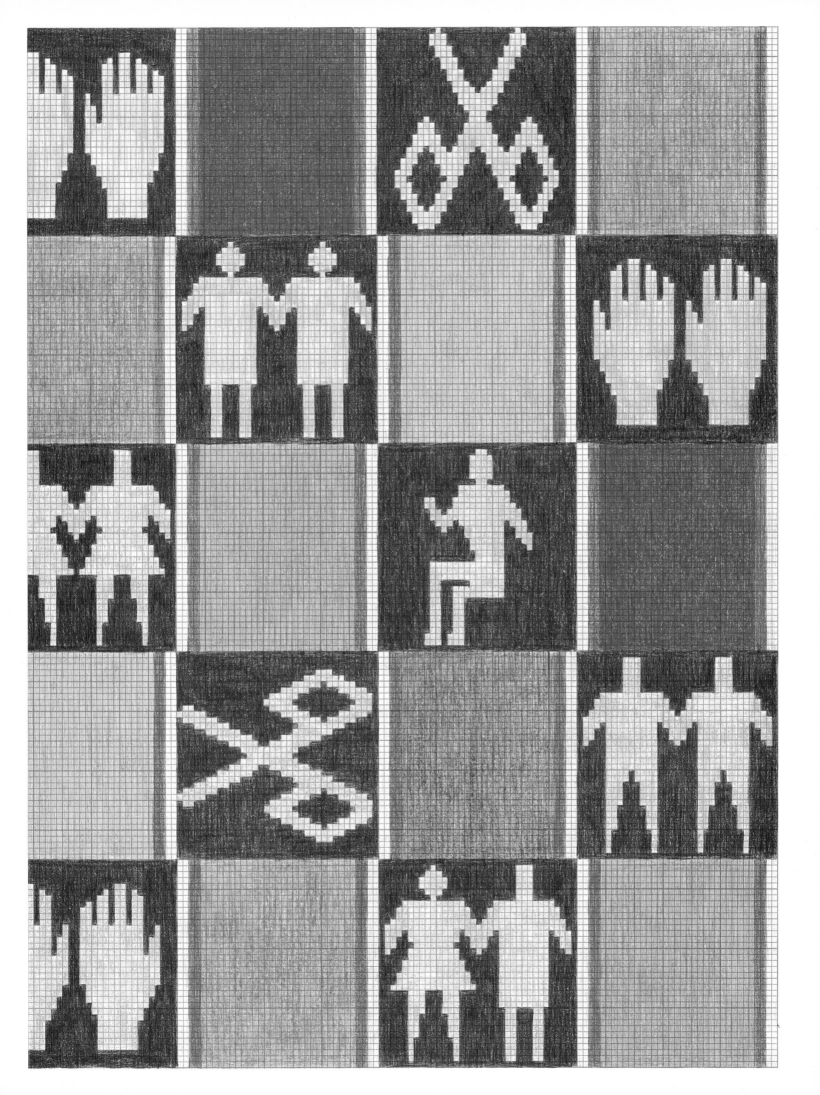

NIGERIAN BLUES

STRIDE OUT INTO THE HEAT OF A SUMMER'S DAY WITH THIS SIMPLE BAG IN SHADES OF INDIGO, RANGING FROM THE DELICATE BLUE OF A MORNING SKY TO A MIDNIGHT NAVY.

The unique process of indigo dyeing has long been associated with Nigeria. Cloth is immersed into indigo dye for a couple of minutes, and when it is first removed from the dye-pot it is green, but as it oxidizes it rapidly deepens to blue. This sequence is repeated, and with each dip the blue is strengthened until finally an intense black is achieved.

Thinking of my wool basket as an indigo dye pot, I dipped into it and chose eight different shades of blue, added cream and a hint of terracotta and worked all these into a simple pattern taken from a piece of African weaving, which I greatly enlarged for a bolder design.

Nigerian Blues chart

MATERIALS

Yarn Appleton tapestry wool in the following approximate amounts.

Bag

	882	102 yd/93 m
	852	20 yd/18 m
	866	50 yd/46 m
	822	24 yd/46 m
	354	22 yd/20 m
	567	14 yd/13 m
	564	26 yd/24 m
	462	26 yd/24 m
	481	18 yd/16 m
	746	16 yd/15 m

Canvas: 12-mesh, single mesh canvas. $27\frac{1}{2}''/69$ cm × $16\frac{1}{2}''/42$ cm.

Finishing material: $\frac{1}{2}$ yd/50 cm of fabric and matching thread. Cord.

Charted design area
284 stitches wide by 152 stitches high.

Finished design
$24''/61$ cm × $12\frac{1}{2}''/32$ cm.

ORDER OF WORK

For full practical information on methods used in order of work, refer to Needlepoint Techniques (pages 150–54). Prepare the canvas. The entire design is worked in half-cross stitch using 1 strand of yarn throughout. Each square on the chart represents one stitch on the canvas. The 142-stitch width given on the chart is just one side of the bag. Repeat once more for the other side. (This gives a total width of 284 stitches.) Stretch the finished needlepoint before trimming the excess canvas to $\frac{1}{2}''/1$ cm. Fold needlepoint in half lengthways with wrong sides together and join seam using half-cross stitch (page 152). Cut a $7\frac{1}{2}''/19$ cm diameter circle of finishing fabric adding $\frac{1}{2}''/1$ cm seam allowance for the base of the bag. Using small backstitch or a sewing machine, stitch the lower edge of the bag to the circular base. Clip seam allowance at regular intervals around the edge.

 Cut a strip of fabric $7\frac{1}{2}''/19$ cm wide by $25''/63$ cm long for the top of the bag. Join width ends of strip together leaving a $1''/2.5$ cm opening, $\frac{1}{2}''/1.5$ cm from one edge. With right sides facing, stitch the top of the bag along the edge of the fabric opposite to the opening. Fold fabric in half to the inside of the bag. Turn a $\frac{1}{2}''/1.5$ cm seam allowance along edge of fabric to wrong side and pin to needlepoint. Stitch neatly in place. Work two rows of stitching along fabric (working through both layers) to form a casing for the cord: one row just above the top of the needlepoint and the other $1''/2.5$ cm above this (i.e. in line with top of seam opening). Cut cord to desired length through casing and knot ends.

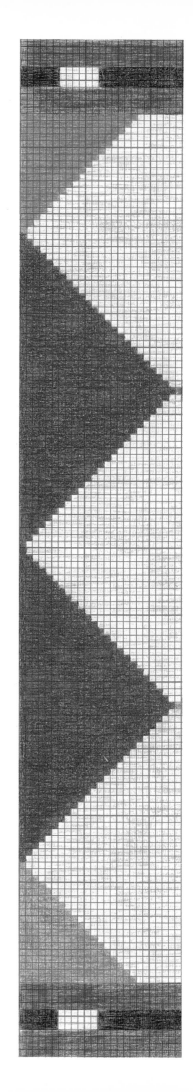

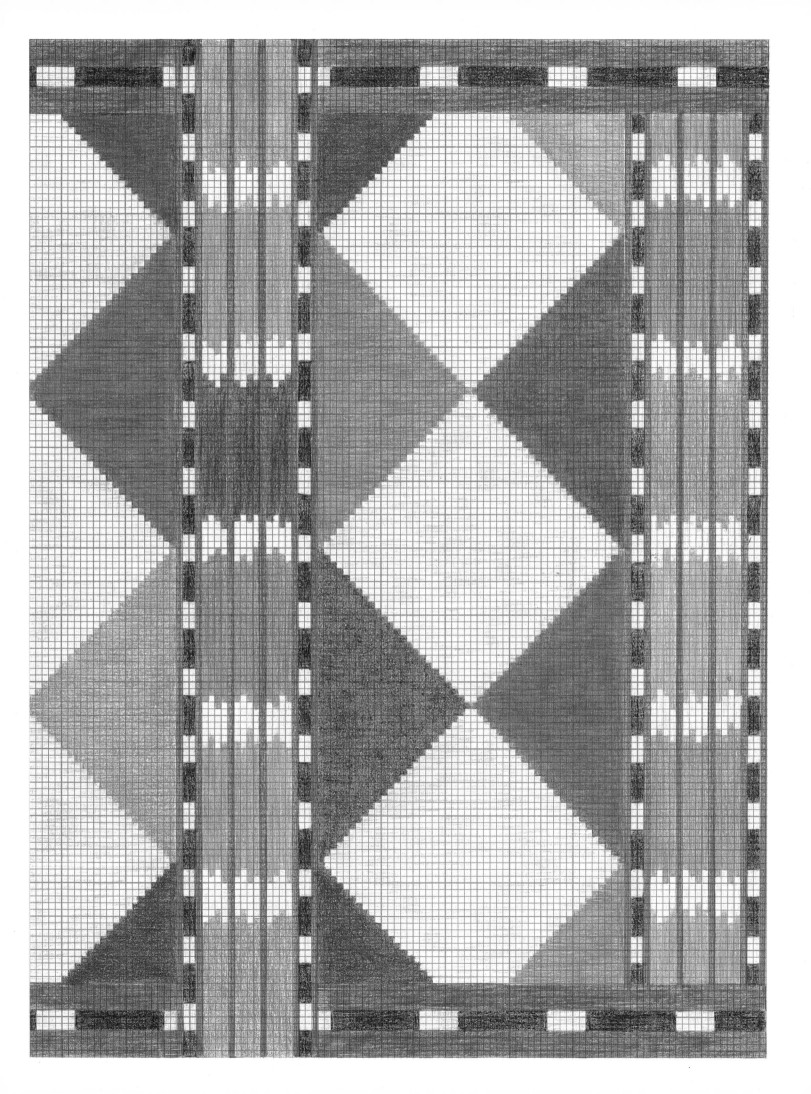

SAHARA CIRCLE

To the African, Even His Basket is an Outlet of Artistic Expression.

Long before the first pottery was made the tribes of Africa were weaving baskets for storage, transport and even cooking. They are still made today, using raffia palms and woven with strong simple designs that seem to echo the austerity of the life of the tribesman, even though there is often little to inspire their patterns.

I plundered my collection of African baskets for a simple repetitive pattern. I particularly like this one; it looks as though it is slowing down from a frantic spin. I kept to the circular format and chose two very different colourways. For the first (on the previous page) I wanted to use colours reminiscent of the desert – faded pinks, sandstone yellow, soft browns with touches of blue, green and very dark brown. For the second colourway I chose stronger colours more typical of West African weaving – orange, burgundy, biscuit, purple and green, contrasting boldly with cream and indigo blue.

If you are using this design on a chair with a hard surface and want a crisp effect, I recommend you use a thick foam for the cushion pad as I have done. For a softer and thicker cushion, when backing the finished needlepoint, make a boxed cushion with a gusset as for Mexican Stars (see order of work page 126).

Sahara Circle chart

MATERIALS

Yarn Appleton tapestry wool in the following colours and approximate amounts.

Cushion: colourway 1

	588	26 yd/24 m
	225	55 yd/50 m
	766	10 yd/9 m
	205	10 yd/9 m
	903	10 yd/9 m
	694	30 yd/27 m
	851	29 yd/26 m
	156	20 yd/18 m

Cushion: colourway 2

	928	53 yd/48 m
	525	24 yd/22 m
	851	47 yd/43 m
	605	10 yd/9 m
	146	17 yd/16 m
	765	10 yd/9 m
	241	19 yd/17 m
	626	11 yd/10 m

Canvas: 12-mesh single canvas 19″/48 cm.

Finishing materials: $\frac{1}{2}$ yd/50 cm backing fabric and matching thread. 12″/30 cm zip fastener. $14\frac{1}{2}$″/37 cm square of $1\frac{1}{2}$″/3 cm thick foam for cushion pad. 46″/117 cm of cord for edging (optional).

Charted design area
181 stitches wide by 181 stitches high.

Finished design
15″/38 cm diameter.

ORDER OF WORK

For full information on methods used in order of work refer to Needlepoint Techniques (pages 150–54). Prepare the canvas. The entire design is worked in half-cross stitch using 1 strand of yarn throughout. Each square on the chart represents one stitch on the canvas. Following the chart, complete the design, working in either colourway 1, as given with the chart, or in colourway 2, by referring to the photograph. Stretch the finished needlepoint before backing. Sew on cord if required.

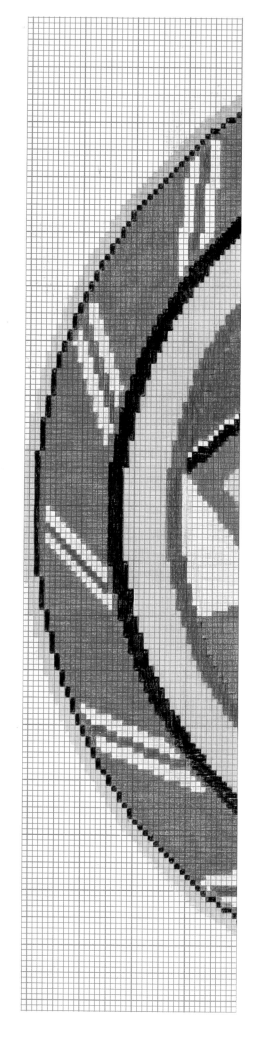

CONGO GRAPHICS

AFRICAN DESIGNS WOVEN AND PRINTED ON CLOTH DUPLICATE THOSE FOUND ON WOOD CARVINGS, ON JEWELLERY, IN HOUSE DECORATION AND BODY MARKING.

Simple geometric motifs and powerful repetitive patterns are abundant in African art. It is the wonderful graphic Raphia textiles made by the Kupa people living on the banks of the Congo in Zaire that appeal to me the most and were indeed the inspiration for these frames. I wanted to capture the graphic simplicity of these patterns, so I designed each frame in combinations of either black and white or black and ochre. Geometric patterns are ideal for anyone wishing to explore their own choice of colours.

Congo Graphics chart

MATERIALS

Yarn Appleton tapestry wool in the following colours and approximate amounts.

Picture frame 1

| | 588 | 27 yd/25 m |
| | 882 | 15 yd/14 m |

Picture frame 2

| | 588 | 35 yd/31 m |
| | 765 | 18 yd/16 m |

Picture frame 3

| | 588 | 42 yd/38 m |
| | 882 | 21 yd/19 m |

Canvas: 12-mesh interlocked canvas. Picture frames 1 and 2. 12½"/32 cm × 10½"/27 cm.
Picture frame 3. 12"/32 cm × 12"/32 cm.

Finishing materials: Stiff cardboard. Masking tape.

Charted design area
Picture frame 1. 93 stitches wide by 116 stitches high.
Picture frame 2. 99 stitches wide by 124 stitches high.
Picture frame 3. 119 stitches wide by 119 stitches high.

Finished design
Picture frame 1. 8"/20 cm × 9½"/24 cm.
Picture frame 2. 8¼"/21 cm × 10¼"/26 cm.
Picture frame 3. 10"/25 cm × 10"/25 cm.

ORDER OF WORK

(Order of work is the same for all three picture frames.) For full practical information on methods used in order of work, refer to Needlepoint Techniques (pages 150–54). Prepare the canvas. The entire design is worked in half-cross stitch using 1 strand of yarn throughout. Each square on the chart represents one stitch on the canvas. Following the chart, complete the design. Stretch the finished needlepoint before making into a frame (see page 154).

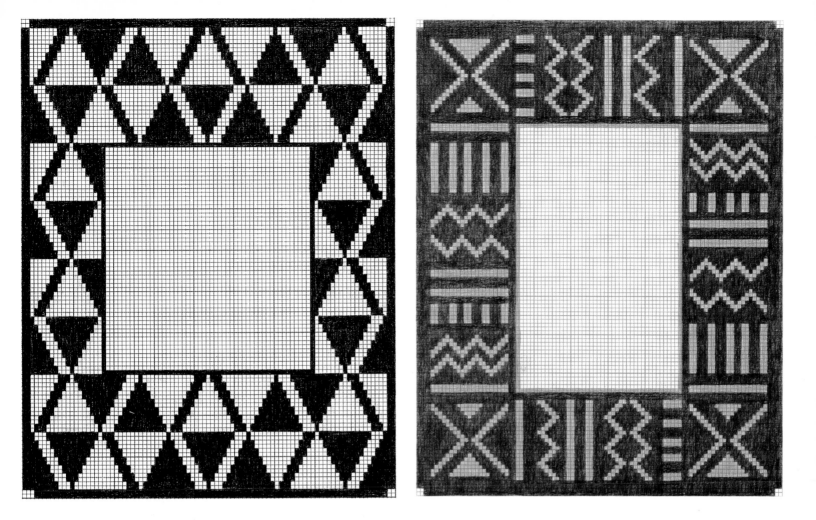

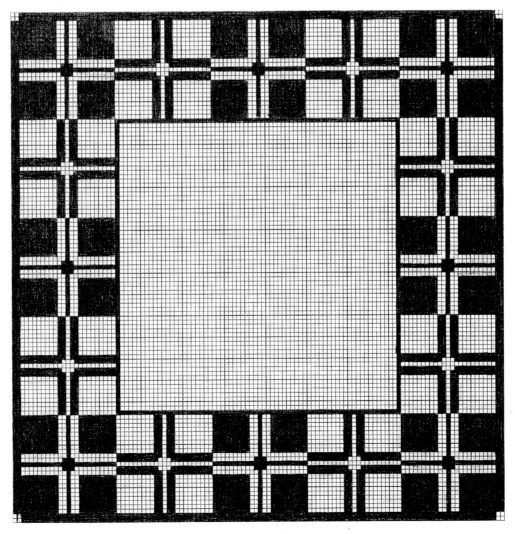

MOROCCAN DIAMONDS

THE BREATHTAKING COLOURS OF MOROCCO OFTEN USED IN STARTLING COMBINATIONS ARE ECHOED IN THE CHOICE OF COLOURS FOR THIS DAZZLING CHAIR AND CUSHION DESIGN.

In the high pastures of the Atlas mountains of Morocco it is easy, particularly in the summer, to miss the tents of the Berber nomads. Woven predominantly in black and brown they blend in with the parched landscape, becoming totally camouflaged. In complete contrast to these tents are the vibrant colours of their rugs, blankets, saddlebags, capes and shawls which are dominated by vivid oranges and sunset reds, with soft mauves and apple greens, yellow ochre, pinks, white and black. Colour for the Berber is associated with extraordinary power. Blue and black protect against the evil eye, as does red, which has additional healing and magical properties. Green is the symbol of prosperity and yellow of health. White, like the gleam of silver, is a good omen and is used particularly for ceremonies.

Immersing myself in the wild colour combinations of Morocco and using the commonly found diamond-within-diamond motif, I created this striking design in contrast to some of my more intricate and subtle patterns from Asia. The colours of both colourways are the same but used in dramatically different ways; for the cushion black is the predominant colour whilst for the chair, it is red, with only a hint of black. If you do not wish to make the chair, work two cushions, one in each colourway – they are glorious together.

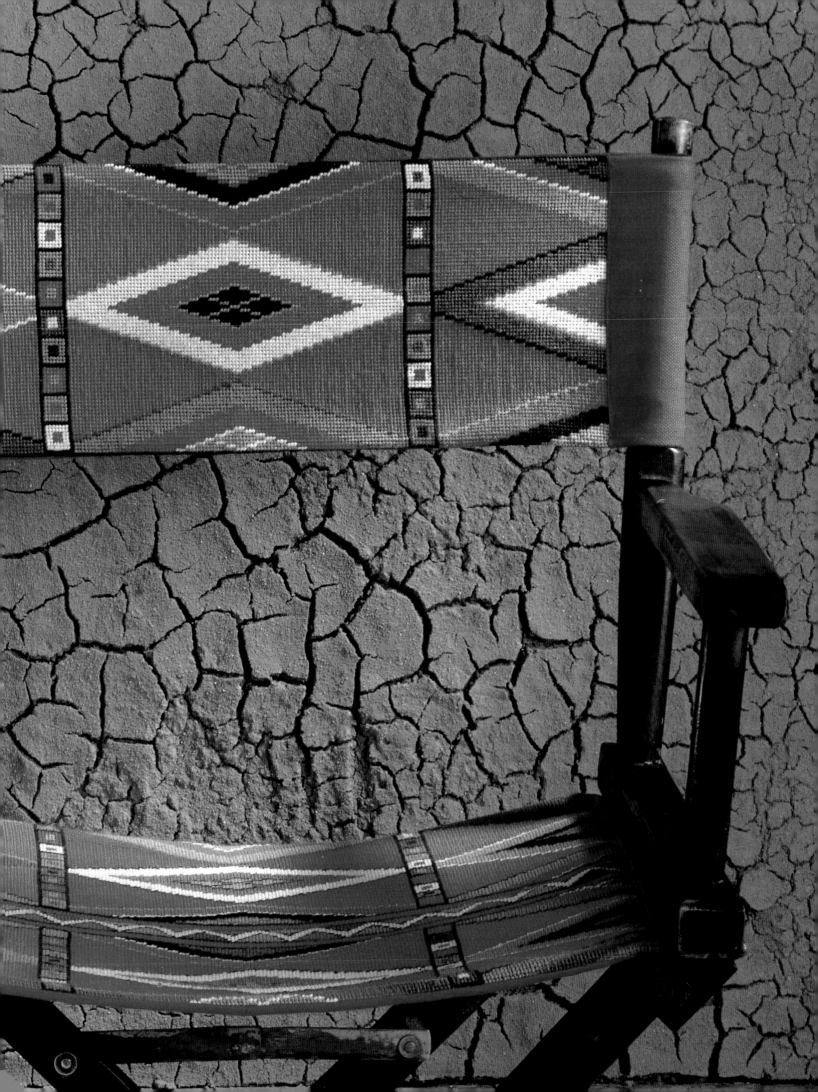

Moroccan Diamonds chart

MATERIALS

Yarn Appleton tapestry wool in the following colours and approximate amounts.

Cushion: colourway 1

Chair: colourway 2

		Seat	Back
998	106 yd/97 m		
882	27 yd/25 m		
446	10 yd/9 m		
994	19 yd/17 m		
475	26 yd/24 m		
242	24 yd/22 m		
605	22 yd/20 m		
946	32 yd/29 m		

		Seat	Back
998	37 yd/34 m	14 yd/13 m
882	33 yd/30 m	12 yd/11 m
446	85 yd/77 m	8 yd/7 m
994	18 yd/16 m	38 yd/35 m
475	20 yd/18 m	11 yd/10 m
242	17 yd/16 m	11 yd/10 m
605	17 yd/16 m	15 yd/14 m
946	25 yd/23 m	15 yd/14 m

Canvas: 12-mesh single canvas.
Cushion: 22"/56 cm × 19½"/49 cm
Chair seat: 22"/56 cm × 19½"/49 cm
Chair back: 22"/56 cm × 11"/28 cm

Finishing materials: Cushion: ½ yd/50 cm of backing fabric and matching thread.
12"/30 cm zip fastener. 69"/175 cm of cord for edging (optional).
Chair seat: ½ yd/50 cm of backing fabric and matching thread.
Chair back: ¼ yd/30 cm of backing fabric and matching thread.

Charted design area
Cushion: 219 stitches wide by 185 stitches high.
Chair seat: 219 stitches wide by 185 stitches high.
Chair back: 219 stitches wide by 83 stitches high.

Finished design
Cushion: 18"/46 cm × 15½"/39 cm
Chair seat: 18"/46 cm × 15½"/39 cm
Chair back: 18"/46 cm × 7"/18 cm

ORDER OF WORK

Cushion For full practical information on methods used in order of work, refer to Needlepoint Techniques (pages 150–54). Prepare the canvas. The entire design is worked in half-cross stitch using 1 strand of yarn throughout. Each square on the chart represents one stitch on the canvas. The chart gives only 104 rows of the design's full 185 row height. For the complete design repeat once more the 81 rows for the diamonds, placing these on the opposite side of the central zig-zag and stripe panel (refer to photograph). Keeping pattern correct, either work colours within diamonds as before or swap them around as I have done for a more random look. For colourway 2 refer to the photograph of the chair. Stretch the finished needlepoint before backing. Sew on cord if required.

Chair seat Following 'order of work' as given for the cushion complete seat, working in either colourway 1 as given with the chart or in colourway 2 by referring to the photograph.

Chair back Following 'order of work' as given for the cushion, work only the 81 rows for the diamonds, omitting central pattern panel (refer to photograph). Stretch both the finished seat and back before backing and assembling on chair.

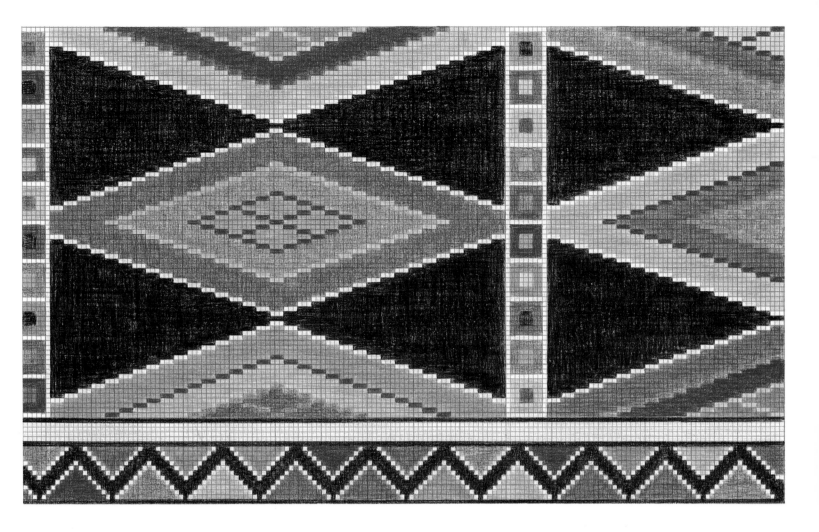

BERBER ARCHES

ADORN YOUR FURNITURE WITH THIS ABSTRACT TRIBAL PATTERN IN GLORIOUS SUN-BAKED COLOURS – A STYLE TYPICAL OF THE PRIZED BERBER RUGS FROM MOROCCO.

As with Moroccan Diamonds (pages 94–9), the dazzling rugs of the Berber nomads were the inspiration for this design. But this time it was the traditional geometric motifs, rather than colour, which was the starting point. Zig-zags, rows of triangles, eight-pointed stars and diamonds are the most frequently used motifs. In contrast to the many richly and symmetrically patterned rugs found in Morocco, Berber rugs are sometimes sparsely decorated and the motifs appear as though just thrown and scattered over a coloured background, or there may be no trace of traditional design and the resulting rug looks more like an abstract expressionist painting.

To complement the chunky shape of this simple footstool, I wanted a large pattern repeat and bolder stitching so I used a coarser 7-mesh canvas. But working on a finer canvas, 12- or 13-mesh, thus reducing the scale of the pattern by half, will offer more possibilities for use. Repeat patterns can be extended indefinitely and used to cover almost any style or size of furniture, making it perfect for dining chairs, piano- and foot-stools and ottomans. This design also offers endless scope for colourways. For something fresh, why not try it in shades of blue with cream, as used for both Nigerian Blues (pages 80–83) and Scissors and Ladies (pages 72–9), or choose the muted colours of the second colourway of Peruvian Swordsmen (pages 134–41).

Berber Arches chart

MATERIALS

Yarn Appleton tapestry wool in the following colours and approximate amounts.

Footstool

	584	26 yd/24 m
	851	40 yd/36 m
	241	24 yd/22 m
	866	30 yd/27 m
	994	22 yd/20 m
	726	14 yd/13 m
	226	28 yd/26 m
	183	18 yd/16 m

Canvas: 7-mesh single canvas 16"/41 cm square.

Finishing materials: Upholstery tacks. 50"/127 cm of braid (optional).

Charted design area
87 stitches wide by 87 stitches high.

Finished design
12"/30 cm square.

ORDER OF WORK

For full practical information on methods used in order of work, refer to Needlepoint Techniques (pages 150–54). Prepare the canvas. The entire design is worked in half-cross stitch using 2 strands of yarn throughout. Each square on the chart represents one stitch on the canvas. Following the chart, complete the design. Stretch the finished needlepoint. Tack down the edges, pulling the needlepoint tight across the stool and positioning upholstery tacks as near as possible to the edges of the design. Cut excess canvas. Either stitch or paste on braid.

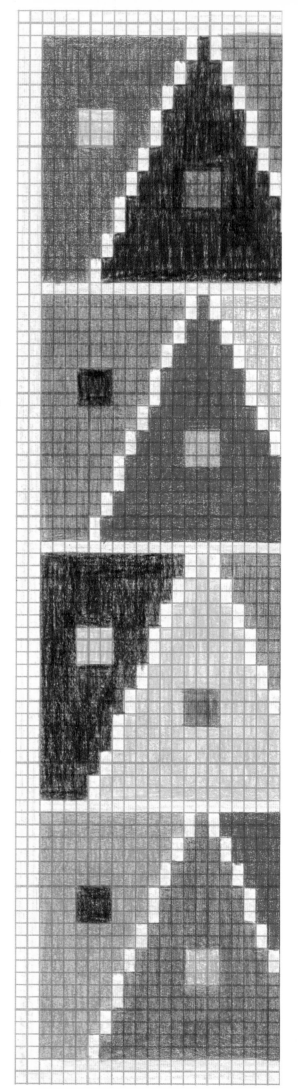

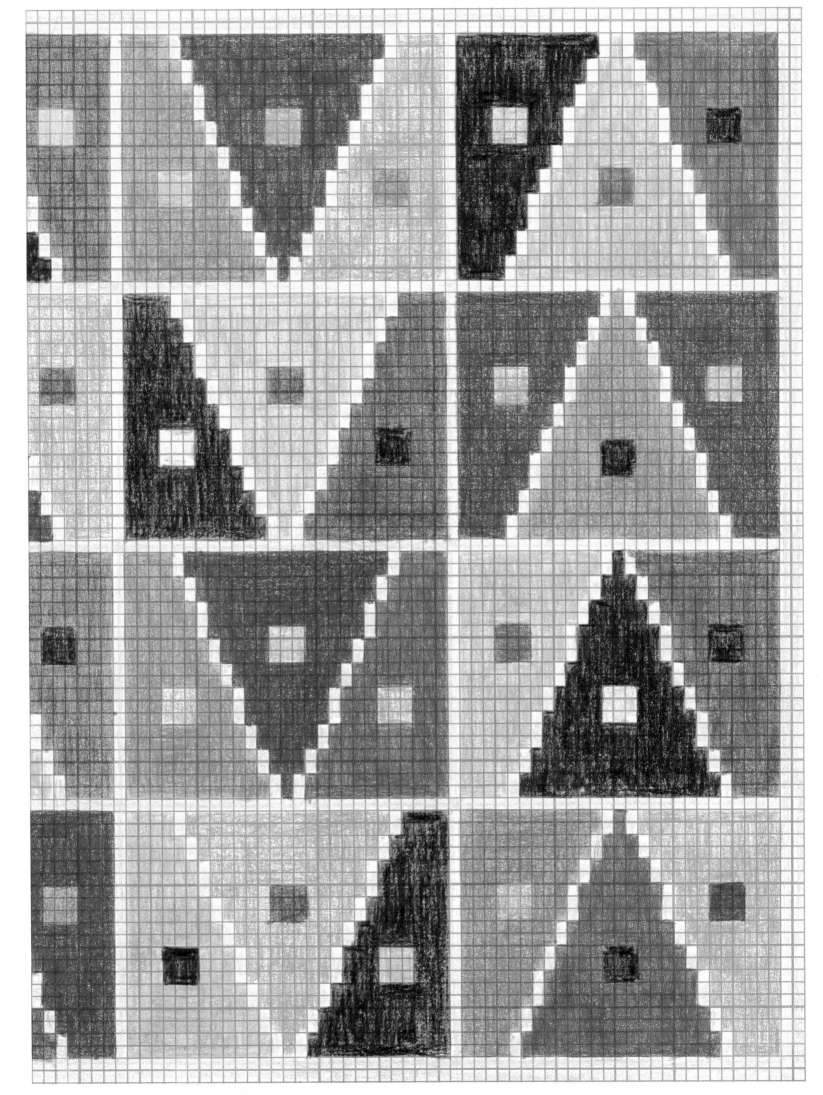

The
Americas

As a child I loved to hear the story of Christopher Columbus, the Spanish explorer, sailing across the Atlantic – the 'sea of Darkness' – in search of a western sea-route to India and finding instead a new world, the gigantic continent of America inhabited by various Indian tribes and their kingdoms. But the story always stopped there and never went on to include the dramatic and dominating influence of these Spanish empire-builders. They condemned what they saw as savage and pagan customs and imposed Christianity. Personal adornment by face and body painting was banned and the Indians were forced to wear European-style dress. Within a few decades of the invasion the great cities had decayed and the art of the ancient Indians had disappeared.

The Indians were now expected to pay taxes. These were collected in the form of cloth for export to Europe or for the settlers' own use. However, with the pagan ceremonies banned, the vast production of ceremonial textiles came to an end. But, in spite of this, weaving for family and domestic use continued (and still does today) as an important aspect of village life. The Spanish introduced new materials, textile techniques and design motifs, and the fabrics became an intriguing mix of Indian and Spanish skills and traditions.

A country which adapted well to these influences was Mexico. With the availability of commercially produced and ready-dyed yarn from Spanish trade routes, their textiles became even more patterned with striking colour combinations in shades of lime green, acid yellow and shocking pink. Clothing was, and still is, brocaded and embroidered to excess with geometric motifs, stylized animals and birds, and an abundance of large flowers; blouses sometimes even resembled miniature flower gardens. This decorative impact was further enhanced by the fusion of pagan and Christian culture that can be seen at its most striking form in the Mexican celebration of death, known as the 'Day of the Dead'. This is when people pay respect to their ancestors, and families set up altars in their homes, adorning them with candles, fruit, flowers and images of saints. Incense is burnt, food and drink offered and ornamental skeletons are bizarrely dressed. Everything is mixed together in a riot of gaudy colours and imagery.

South of Mexico, in the highland villages of

Guatemala, the strong tradition of weaving also continues, and many pre-conquest designs and motifs are still in use, such as the snake, the double-headed bird, and the sun and moon motifs, as well as many of the animals. Horses, peacocks and chickens are more recent elements, these animals being introduced by the Spanish. They are all embroidered as well as woven into stylized shapes and combined with flowers and abstract motifs in an undiluted but sophisticated use of colour.

In spite of the introduction of more advanced weaving equipment by the Spanish, the simplest of looms, the portable back-strap loom, is still very much in use throughout Mexico, Guatemala and Peru. Of ancient origin, it consists essentially of two end-sticks which support the vertical warp threads. One of these sticks is roped to a post or tree, while a strap is attached to the other. This strap is passed around the weaver's hips so that the tension can be controlled by moving the body. The weaver usually sits on the ground to work and uses a batten to beat the weft threads down after they have been passed through the warp threads with a shuttle. The length and width of cloth depend on the reach and strength of the weaver.

Of the many ancient cultures of Peru to have influenced my work the Inca Empire is probably the most famous. Figurative forms were banished by the Christian invaders, and so the Incas created textiles that were superbly woven with some of the finest and most sophisticated geometric patterns ever, and whose quality and quantity astonished the Spanish. Peruvian textiles today are woven mainly in cotton and the wool of native alpaca or llama and are used for ponchos, ceremonial wraps, sashes and braid. In contrast with their spartan and simple lifestyle, their weaving is richly decorated, using colours of startling brightness.

All the countries of Central and South America are a great source of inspiration. In addition to Peru, Mexico and Guatemala, there is Bolivia, Ecuador, Panama, each with its own style. Look not just at the textiles, as I have done here, but also at the furniture, the ceramics (in particular the tiles) and the buildings, often with a strong Spanish influence and painted in dazzling colour combinations. Nowhere is the decorative impact so strong nor the styles so diverse as in the American continent, the great melting pot of cultures.

GUATEMALAN DOGS

THE INDIANS OF GUATEMALA DRAW UPON THEIR GREAT LOVE AND RESPECT OF NATURE FOR INSPIRATION, DECORATING THEIR COSTUMES WITH BIRDS, ANIMALS AND PLANT FORMS.

Hens, peacocks, dogs, horses, pine trees and corn plants are all combined with numerous geometric shapes to create glorious intricate patterns. These are woven and embroidered in colours dyed to a startling and intoxicating brightness.

To imitate this combination of realistic and geometric forms, I combined rows of dogs with diamonds and zig-zags but, rather than using the typical dazzling colours of Guatemala, I chose mellow colours more reminiscent of the Caucasian carpet.

Guatemalan Dogs chart

MATERIALS

Yarn Appleton tapestry wool in the following colours and approximate amounts.

Cushion

■	155	61 yd/56 m
■	588	14 yd/13 m
□	691	19 yd/17 m
■	504	26 yd/24 m
■	226	27 yd/25 m
■	714	27 yd/25 m
■	605	15 yd/14 m
■	696	28 yd/26 m
■	242	14 yd/13 m

Canvas: 12-mesh single canvas 19"/48 cm square.

Finishing materials: ½ yd/50 cm of backing fabric and matching thread. 12"/30 cm zip fastener. 62"/157 cm of cord for edging (optional).

Charted design area
179 stitches wide by 179 stitches high.

Finished design
15"/38 cm square.

ORDER OF WORK

For full practical information on methods used in order of work, refer to Needlepoint Techniques (pages 150–54). Prepare the canvas. The entire design is worked in half-cross stitch using 1 strand of yarn throughout. Each square on the chart represents one stitch on the canvas. Following the chart, complete the design. Stretch the finished needlepoint before backing. Sew on cord if required.

ANDEAN WINGS

INFLUENCED BY THE MYSTERIOUS IMAGERY OF ANCIENT PERUVIAN ART, THIS BOLD DESIGN ONLY DIPS INTO THE WEALTH OF DISTINCTIVE SHAPES AND BEAUTIFUL COLOURS TO BE FOUND WOVEN INTO THEIR LAVISH TEXTILES.

From the many different pre-Columbian cultures of Peru have come some of the finest textiles, many perfectly preserved in burials by an ideal combination of dry climate and sandy soil. One of the most famous of these was the Tiahuanaco culture which originated in the highlands of the central Andes. The peoples connected with this culture wove exquisite textiles often using hundreds of different colours and patterning their work with either figurative motifs drawn from the decorated stone monuments of their great cities or with very formal arrangements consisting of the 'diagonal-double motif' – a rectangle containing pairs of abstract elements divided by a diagonal line. The ancient Peruvians frequently used this motif in the weaving of their poncho shirts.

In this design I used the diagonal-double motif but simplified it by using just one element, a stepped spiral – a shape thought to have originated from the bird wing. This pattern offers inexhaustible scope for playing with colour and I worked it in just two variations. For this first I chose several shades of red and brown with highlights of yellow and cream for a rich, harmonious and typically Peruvian combination, and for the other, an abundance of bright colours, more typical of Guatemala.

Andean Wings chart

MATERIALS

Yarn Appleton tapestry wool in the following colours and approximate amounts.

Cushion: colourway 1

Cushion: colourway 2

	Colourway 1			Colourway 2
	584	72 yd/66 m		822	35 yd/32 m
	226	28 yd/26 m		454	19 yd/17 m
	504	27 yd/25 m		801	17 yd/16 m
	724	32 yd/29 m		446	37 yd/34 m
	994	26 yd/24 m		864	20 yd/18 m
	695	32 yd/29 m		946	12 yd/11 m
	183	28 yd/26 m		894	18 yd/16 m
	851	25 yd/23 m		525	16 yd/15 m
				241	13 yd/12 m
				882	24 yd/22 m
				474	14 yd/13 m

Canvas: 12-mesh single canvas 20"/50 cm × 18"/45 cm.

Finishing materials: $\frac{1}{2}$ yd/50 cm of backing fabric and matching thread. 12"/50 cm zip fastener. 62"/157 cm of cord for edging (optional).

Charted design area
190 stitches wide by 170 stitches high.

Finished design
16"/41 cm × 14"/36 cm.

ORDER OF WORK

For full practical information on methods used in order of work, refer to Needlepoint Techniques (pages 150–54). Prepare the canvas. The entire design is worked in half-cross stitch using 1 strand of yarn throughout. Each square on the chart represents one stitch on the canvas. Following the chart, complete the design, working in either colourway 1 as given with the chart, or in colourway 2, by referring to the photograph. Stretch the finished needlepoint before backing. Sew on cord if required.

SERRATED DIAMONDS

THE NAVAJO INDIAN WEAVER CELEBRATED THE INTRODUCTION OF SYNTHETIC DYES WITH A COCKTAIL OF SERRATED DIAMONDS AND VIBRANT COLOURS THAT INSPIRED THE CREATION OF THIS 'EYE-DAZZLER'.

It is easy to forget that the various tribal weavers throughout the world did not always have easy access to coloured woven thread. Availability of colour largely depended on what natural dye sources could be found in the surrounding landscape and the opening of trade routes. For a long time the Navajo Indians of the American southwest were limited to weaving with brown, cream and grey, the natural colours of their sheeps' wool, and with indigo blue, a dye introduced to them by the Spanish. Red dye was not available until the late nineteenth century so the Navajo resorted to unravelling Spanish cloth with red thread woven into it. Occasionally small amounts of yellow and green were added.

The introduction of bright synthetic colours brought a revolution to their weaving. Previously limited, they suddenly had the full spectrum of colour to chose from. They started to create optical effects by combining vibrant colours and serrated diamonds and the resulting designs became known as 'eye-dazzlers'. I made this simple folder and covered it with a typical 'eye-dazzler' design, though I chose to tone the colours down a little. This pattern can be extended indefinitely and used to cover cushions and even a complete set of dining chairs.

Serrated Diamonds chart

MATERIALS

Yarn Appleton tapestry wool in the following colours and approximate amounts.

Folder

■	588	39 yd/36 m
■	866	26 yd/24 m
■	726	12 yd/11 m
■	474	15 yd/14 m
□	882	12 yd/11 m

Canvas: 12-mesh interlocked canvas 11″/28 cm × 14″/35 cm.

Finishing materials: A piece of backing fabric 12½″/31.5 cm square. Two pieces of 2 mm thick cardboard 9″/23 cm × 10½″/26.5 cm. One piece of thinner cardboard or heavy paper 18″/45.5 cm × 10½″/26.5 cm. Masking tape. Strong glue.

Charted design area
95 stitches wide by 125 stitches high.

Finished design
8″/20 cm × 10½″/26.5 cm.

Completed folder
9″/23 cm wide by 10½″/26.5 cm high.

ORDER OF WORK

For full practical information on methods used in order of work, refer to Needlepoint Techniques (pages 150–54). Prepare the canvas. The entire design is worked in half-cross stitch using 1 strand of yarn throughout. Each square on the chart represents one stitch on the canvas. Following the chart, complete the design. Stretch the finished needlepoint before backing. Do not cut excess canvas at this stage. Stitch backing fabric to needlepoint along one side edge. Trim seam. Press. With masking tape join the two pieces of 2 mm thick cardboard along one side edge, taping on both sides to form a spine. Position cardboard piece open over back of needlepoint and backing fabric. Trim the excess canvas and fabric leaving a 1″/2.5 cm overlap all round. Cut the corners diagonally. Fold all overlap over card to inside and tape or glue securely in place. Position the thinner card or heavy paper for the inside of the folder over the back of the front piece. Glue into position. Place under a heavy object to dry for at least an hour. On the inside of the folder gently score down the centre of lining card to mark spine. Fold in half.

MEXICAN STARS

THESE LUMINOUS CUSHIONS IN A RIOT OF COLOUR ECHO THE EXUBERANT SPIRIT OF MEXICAN DESIGN.

In defiance of an arid and monochrome landscape, the Mexicans have developed a dramatic vocabulary of colour that is totally uninhibited and full of cheerful impact. The houses, streets, ceramics, tiles and textiles all display bold, simple colours used with sheer inventiveness – acid yellow, cobalt blue, scarlet, magenta, orange and violet – all in vibrant combinations unique to Mexico.

Lifting motifs from various Mexican Indian textiles, the widely used triangle, the sun and the star, I designed three dramatic circular cushions. To convey the bold style of Mexican colour was my starting point. Many people might find these cushions too bright. I urge you to make them – adorn your garden with them in the summer and in the evening light they will shimmer even more vividly.

Mexican Stars chart – variation 1

MATERIALS

Yarn Appleton tapestry wool in the following colours and approximate amounts.

Cushion: colourway 1

■	464	27 yd/25 m
■	483	29 yd/26 m
■	453	25 yd/23 m
■	476	28 yd/26 m
■	554	22 yd/20 m
■	995	31 yd/28 m
■	802	5 yd/5 m

Cushion: colourway 2

■	464	37 yd/34 m
■	483	31 yd/28 m
■	453	26 yd/24 m
■	476	34 yd/31 m
■	554	36 yd/33 m
■	995	7 yd/6 m

Canvas: 12-mesh single canvas $17\frac{1}{2}$"/44 cm square.

Finishing materials: $\frac{1}{2}$ yd/50 cm of backing fabric and matching thread. 10"/25 cm zip fastener.

Charted design area
162 stitches wide by 162 stitches high.

Finished design
$13\frac{1}{2}$/35 cm diameter.

ORDER OF WORK

For full practical information on methods used in order of work, refer to Needlepoint Techniques (pages 150–54). Prepare the canvas. The entire design is worked in half-cross stitch using 1 strand of yarn throughout. Each square on the chart represents one stitch on the canvas. Following the chart, complete the design, working in either colourway 1 as given with the chart or in colourway 2, by referring to the photograph. Stretch the finished needlepoint before backing. For the gusset, cut a stripe of 3"/8 cm-wide backing fabric to fit the circumference of your finished needlepoint adding $\frac{5}{8}$"/1.5 cm at both ends for seam allowance. Join ends, stitch one edge of gusset to needlepoint. For the base, cut out piece of fabric the area of the needlepoint, adding $\frac{5}{8}$"/1.5 cm seam allowance all round. (If using zip fastener see page 152). Stitch second edge of gusset to cushion base. Clip all seam allowances at regular intervals around the edge before turning cover out.

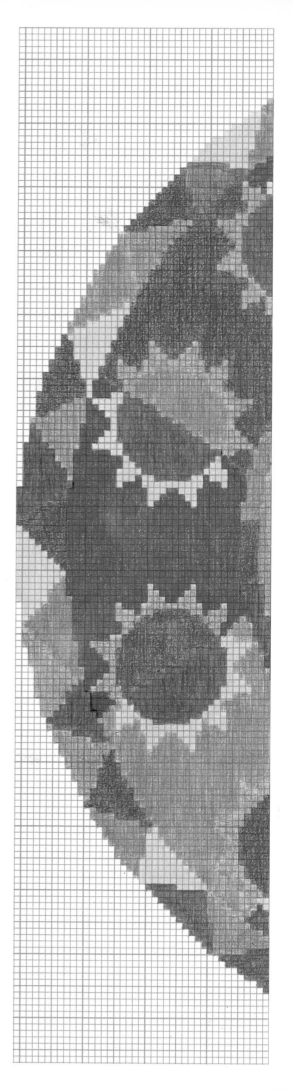

Mexican Stars chart – variation 2

MATERIALS

Yarn Appleton tapestry wool in the following colours and approximate amounts

Cushion

■	464	36 yd/33 m
■	483	29 yd/26 m
■	453	23 yd/21 m
■	476	27 yd/25 m
■	554	28 yd/26 m
■	995	17 yd/16 m

Canvas: 12-mesh single canvas $17\frac{1}{2}$"/44 cm square.

Finishing materials: $\frac{1}{2}$ yd/50 cm of backing fabric and matching thread. 10"/25 cm zip fastener.

Charted design area
158 stitches wide by 158 stitches high.

Finished design
13"/33 cm diameter.

ORDER OF WORK

For full practical information on methods used in order of work, refer to Needlepoint Techniques (pages 150–54). Prepare the canvas. The entire design is worked in half-cross stitch using 1 strand of yarn throughout. Each square on the chart represents one stitch on the canvas. Following the chart, complete the design. Stretch the finished needlepoint before backing. For the gusset, cut a stripe of 3"/8 cm-wide backing fabric to fit the circumference of your finished needlepoint adding $\frac{5}{8}$"/1.5 cm at both ends for seam allowance. Join ends, stitch one edge of gusset to needlepoint. For the base, cut out piece of fabric the area of the needlepoint, adding $\frac{5}{8}$"/1.5 cm seam allowance all round. (If using zip fastener see page 152). Stitch second edge of gusset to cushion base. Clip all seam allowances at regular intervals around the edge before turning cover out.

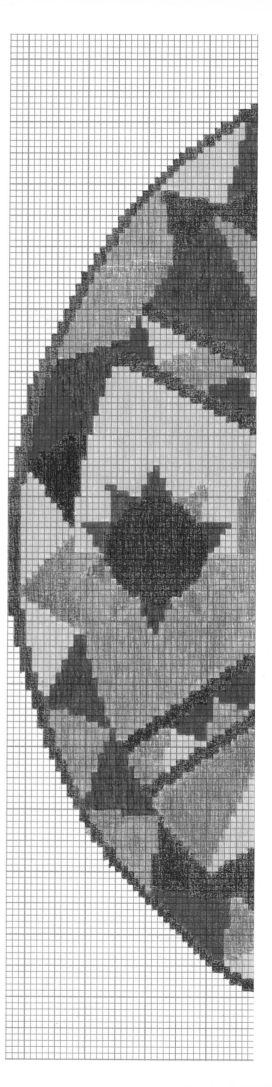

MOUNTAIN BROCADE

LIGHT UP A CHILD'S ROOM WITH THIS STRIKING LAMPSHADE IN A SIMPLE MIX OF GUATEMALAN PATTERN AND COLOUR.

In the highland villages of Guatemala there still thrives a long tradition of weaving, brocading and embroidery. These textiles are used mainly for clothing and are intricately patterned with combinations of realistic animals, birds and figures mixed with geometric motifs, many of which survive from pre-Columbian times. Although the same distinctive motifs are used throughout Guatemala, each village has evolved its own unique combination of colour and design in the same way as each village differs in the way a ribbon is worn, a belt tied or a skirt arranged. There is no better place to see this intoxicating mix of patterned costumes, each bearing its own personal touch, than on market day or at a festival.

In designing Mountain Brocade my first priority was to find a motif or pattern that would work well with the shape of the lampshade. This I found in the brocaded yoke of a child's blouse. I greatly simplified the pattern but kept the strongest elements: the widely used diamond and triangle shapes and the random use of colour. Although we associate Guatemala with the most vibrant of undiluted colour combinations, the unusual, more subdued mix used for this lampshade is just as common. This design would be wonderful for a child's room and because of its simplicity, would be an ideal first piece for someone to do. It is also a useful design for using up odd bits of yarn.

Mountain Brocade chart

MATERIALS

Yarn Appleton tapestry wool in the following colours and approximate amounts.

Lampshade

☐	882	15 yd/14 m
▨	998	16 yd/15 m
▨	474	6 yd/5 m
▨	821	19 yd/17 m
▨	946	24 yd/22 m
▨	526	14 yd/13 m
▨	454	13 yd/12 m
▨	147	13 yd/12 m
▨	693	14 yd/13 m

Canvas: 12-mesh interlocked canvas 21"/53 cm × 14"/35 cm.

Finishing materials: Lampshade frame 8"/20 cm diameter × 5"/13 cm high. 38"/97 cm of cord for edging (optional). Lining paper.

Charted design area
201 stitches wide by 100 stitches high.

Finished design
17"/43 cm × 8"/20 cm.

ORDER OF WORK

For full practical information on methods used in order of work, refer to Needlepoint Techniques (pages 150–54). Prepare the canvas. The entire design is worked in half-cross stitch using 1 strand of yarn throughout. Each square on the chart represents one stitch on the canvas. Following the chart, complete the design. Stitch the finished needlepoint. Trim the excess canvas. Join the two straight edges using small backstitches and then sew to frame. Line the shade with paper and trim top and bottom with cord if required.

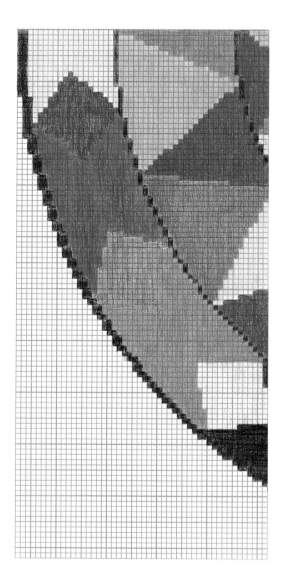

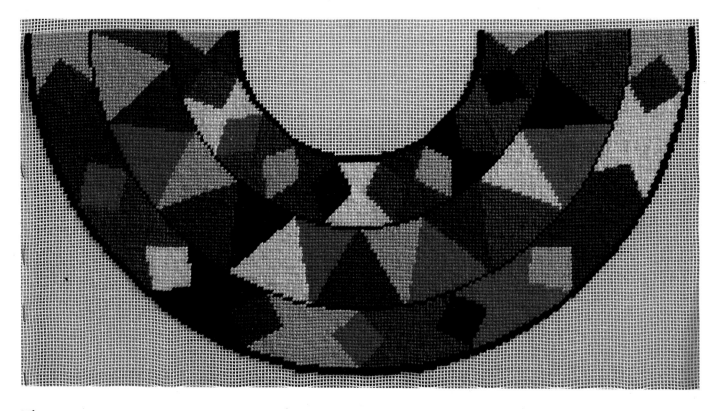

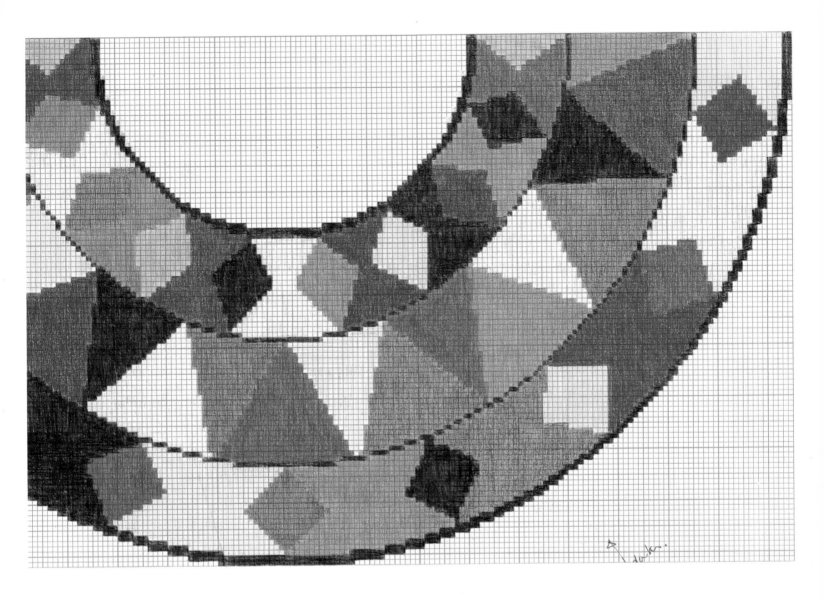

PERUVIAN SWORDSMEN

THE FIGURES OF THE PERUVIAN DESIGNS FOUND IN THE STONE CARVINGS OF THEIR GREAT CITIES ARE REPEATED IN THEIR EXQUISITE TEXTILES.

For Peruvian Swordsmen I turned once again to the ancient cultures of Peru for inspiration. In contrast to the abstract textile patterns which I explored for my cushion design, Andean Wings on pages 114–19, I chose this time to plunder the great variety of highly stylized figures to be found – humans, monkey-like creatures, fish, snakes and frogs are the most common. Each of these figurative motifs, usually arranged in rows, is composed of a patchwork of small geometric shapes – a style typical of much Peruvian art in various forms, not just in its textiles but in its ceramics, metalwork and sculpture. From this endless display of figures, I chose for my design a simple row of men resembling warriors, with raised hands and wearing headdresses.

For Peruvian Swordsmen I decided on two very different colourways: for the first, as seen in the cushion, a small palette of bright, contrasting colours with purple as the background colour; for the second, used with the director's chair, a harmonious and typically Peruvian mix of browns, rusts and beiges with touches of blue-green. Rather than using the same background colour for both chair back and seat, I used the lightest colour for the back and the darkest for the seat. To the chair seat I added a Peruvian border pattern along the top and bottom edges because I didn't want an endless amount of background colour.

Peruvian Swordsmen chart

MATERIALS

Yarn Appleton tapestry wool in the following colours and approximate amounts.

Cushion: colourway 1

	454	130 yd/118 m
	504	13 yd/12 m
	726	18 yd/16 m
	333	13 yd/12 m
	695	15 yd/14 m
	851	31 yd/28 m
	584	14 yd/13 m

Canvas: 12-mesh single canvas.
Cushion: 17″/43 cm × 16″/40 cm.
Chair seat: 21½″/54 cm × 19″/48 cm.
Chair back: 21½″/54 cm × 11″/27 cm.

Finishing materials: Cushion: ½ yd/50 cm of backing fabric and matching thread.
10″/25 cm zip fastener. 52″/132 cm of cord for edging (optional).
Chair seat: ½ yd/50 cm of backing fabric and matching thread.
Chair back: ¼ yd/30 cm of backing fabric and matching thread.

Charted design area
Cushion: 156 stitches wide by 148 stitches high.
Chair seat: 212 stitches wide by 180 stitches high.
Chair back: 212 stitches wide by 88 stitches high.

Finished design
Cushion: 13″/33 cm × 12″/31 cm.
Chair seat: 17½″/44 cm × 15″/38 cm.
Chair back: 17½″/44 cm × 7″/18 cm.

Chair: colourway 2

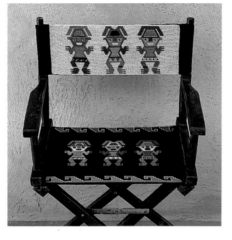

		Back	Seat
	588	3 yd/3 m	151 yd/137 m
	226	12 yd/11 m	28 yd/26 m
	722	9 yd/8 m	9 yd/8 m
	766	6 yd/5 m	25 yd/23 m
	976	12 yd/11 m	3 yd/3 m
	183	3 yd/3 m	8 yd/7 m
	155	8 yd/7 m	8 yd/7 m
	691	107 yd/99 m	19 yd/17 m
	695	3 yd/3 m	3 yd/3 m

ORDER OF WORK

Cushion For full practical information on methods used in order of work, refer to Needlepoint Techniques (pages 150–54). Prepare the canvas. The entire design is worked in half-cross stitch using 1 strand of yarn throughout. Each square on the chart represents one stitch on the canvas. Following the chart, work in either colourway 1 as given with chart or in colourway 2, by referring to the photograph of the chair. When the chart is complete, continue working in background colour only. In addition to the chart work an extra 30 rows above and below the figures and an extra 7 rows on both sides. Stretch the finished needlepoint before backing. Sew on cord if required.

Chair seat Follow order of work as given for the cushion. To increase the width of the design, as set on the chart, not only did I add an extra 18 rows of background colour to each side edge but also moved the swordsmen further apart by adding an extra 10 rows of background colour between each figure. I then added an additional 28 rows above and below before adding a border pattern. This is a 31 stitch repeat and is repeated across top and bottom edges.

Chair back Follow order of work as given for the cushion. Increase the width of the back exactly as for the chair seat. No extra rows of background colour are added above or below the figures. Stretch both the finished seat and back pieces before assembling on chair.

NAVAJO STRIPES

THE STRONG GRAPHIC DESIGNS OF THE
NAVAJO INDIANS, OFTEN WOVEN IN JUST
THREE CLASSIC COLOURS, ARE ECHOED
LOUDLY IN THESE STRIKINGLY SIMPLE
CUSHIONS.

As far as I am concerned, the most visually
exciting of American Indian weaving is the
classic nineteenth-century Navajo blanket. Worn
as wraps, the earliest of these blankets displayed
many different arrangements of stripes. The
rhythm was slowly broken in the mid-century by
the introduction of rectangular blocks of
contrasting colour. These blocks then finally
developed into an overlay of diamonds on the

striped ground with sometimes only the central diamond motif fully visible. These later compositions are the most widely recognized and popular blanket styles and were indeed the springboard for my own design Navajo Stripes.

After the many glorious colours and endless wealth of stimulating design motifs, used throughout this book, it was both refreshing and challenging to limit myself to just three colours: red, navy and cream, and a minimal design composed of stripes, crosses and diamonds – the essence of Navajo design.

For the first, brighter colourway, I alternated the wider stripes in cream and navy. For the second, darker colourway but still using the same three colours, I omitted all the cream stripes so navy, rather than cream, became the dominant colour. Keeping to the same colours, you could try further alternative colourways and create a distinctive collection of graphic cushions.

Navajo Stripes chart

MATERIALS

Yarn Appleton tapestry wool in the following colours and approximate amounts.

Cushion: colourway 1

▨	882	87 yd/79 m
▧	852	52 yd/47 m
▢	866	140 yd/128 m

Cushion: colourway 2

▨	882	39 yd/36 m
▧	852	98 yd/89 m
▢	866	117 yd/107 m

Canvas: 7-mesh single canvas 20″/50 cm square.

Finishing materials: ½ yd/50 cm of backing fabric and matching thread. 12″/30 cm zip fastener. 65″/165 cm of cord for edging (optional).

Charted design area
110 stitches wide by 108 stitches high.

Finished design
16″/40 cm × 15½″/39 cm.

ORDER OF WORK

For full practical information on methods used in order of work, refer to Needlepoint Techniques (pages 150–54). Prepare the canvas. The entire design is worked in half-cross stitch using 2 strands of yarn throughout. Each square on the chart represents one stitch on the canvas. Following the chart, complete the design, working in either colourway 1 as given with the chart or in colourway 2, by referring to the photograph. Stretch the finished needlepoint before backing. Sew on cord if required.

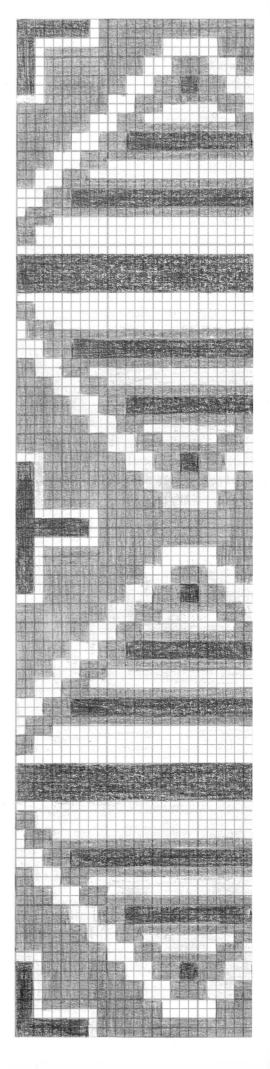

Needlepoint
Techniques

Canvas

There are three types of canvas: single (or mono), interlocked, and double-thread (or Penelope). Single thread canvas is evenly woven using single thread and is ideal for half-cross stitch. It is particularly strong and sturdy. Interlock canvas looks similar to single thread canvas, but instead of the threads passing under and over one another, the threads are twisted so that they lock at the intersection, thus preventing the canvas threads shifting with the tension of the stitches or from fraying around the edges. Double-thread canvas is woven using pairs of threads and stitches are normally worked over both threads. However, by separating the pairs and stitching over one thread only, much finer stitches can be worked. This canvas is ideal for designs where more than one type of stitch is used. Fine stitches used for detail can be combined on the same canvas with larger background stitches.

1. Three canvas types: interlock, single and double-thread.

Most canvas is woven from cotton or linen, and except for interlock, comes in a choice of three colours: white, the most readily available, cream (sometimes called antique) and brown, an unbleached canvas. Interlock is only made in white and therefore far more care has to be taken to cover the canvas well with the stitches to prevent any white thread showing through.

Apart from availability in different types and colours, canvas also comes in a range of sizes, measured by the number of threads or holes per 1"/2.5 cm. This is known as the mesh count. Canvas can come as fine as 32 threads or holes per 1"/2.5 cm, making it ideal for petit-point, or as coarse as 3 threads per 1"/2.5 cm and used for needlepoint rugs. I generally like using a medium mesh size of 12 or 13 holes per 1"/2.5 cm. It is fine enough to create good detail and is perfect for half-cross stitch.

The choice of canvas is a matter of personal taste. Be careful with interlock canvas; unless it is firmly framed during work, it will tend to pull out of shape. Being so fine and pliable it can then be difficult to stretch back, as the canvas will not take a lot of tension without breaking. Keep interlock canvas for the smaller pieces of needlepoint.

When buying canvas, try to buy the best quality you can afford and always buy sufficient to allow at least a 2"/5 cm margin around the finished design.

Yarns

There are three standard needlepoint yarns available: crewel, tapestry and Persian. Crewel yarn is a fine twisted 2-ply yarn and several strands together are needed to cover a 12-mesh canvas. Tapestry wool is thicker than crewel and a single strand will cover a 12- or 13-mesh canvas whilst two strands together will cover a 7-mesh canvas. Persian yarn is made up of three strands and, like crewel yarn, the strands can be easily separated giving the flexibility to use the same yarn on different gauges of canvas as well as to do a variety of stitches on one canvas. In addition, you can mix your own colours by using two or three different coloured strands and threading all together into the one needle. For the purpose of this book, mixing colours and separating strands is not required and for that reason my preference was for tapestry wool.

Whichever yarn you finally choose, it is essential that the yarn is thick enough to cover the canvas thread completely, but not so thick as to create difficulty in passing the threaded needle through the canvas, which results in distorting the canvas weave.

When buying yarns for the needlepoint designs in this book, remember that amounts given are only approximate. The amounts are estimated for half-cross stitch. Basketweave and continental stitch (the two other most popular needlepoint stitches), use nearly twice as much yarn as does half-cross stitch. Amounts of yarn used do also vary from one person to another depending how loosely or tightly you work.

If possible buy all your yarn at one time, particularly yarn for a background or large area worked in one colour. If not possible, keep a record of the dye lot so you can match the colour perfectly.

If you wish to duplicate my needlepoint designs exactly, buy the same brand of a tapestry wool and the same colour number as given with each design. If you wish to substitute yarns of another brand, use the conversion chart on page 155, where I have listed equivalent colour numbers for several of the most popular and readily available needlepoint yarns, or be bold and make your own choices.

Needles

Tapestry needles have large eyes and a rounded point so as not to split the canvas. They are available in a range of sizes from 13–26, the higher the number the smaller the needle. It is important that the eye of the needle is sufficiently large to allow the yarn to pass through easily without fraying. In addition the threaded needle must not be too thick to pass through the canvas, otherwise the canvas threads will be displaced. As a general guide, size 18 is used on 10- and 12-mesh canvas.

Frames

When working on a small canvas it is possible to hold the canvas in one hand while stitching with the other. However, especially when working with a larger canvas, it is advisable to use a frame. Without a frame the canvas can be pulled out of shape, particularly if you tend to stitch too tightly. Working with a frame also leaves both hands free so that one hand may be used above and the other one below the canvas, allowing the needle to pass back and forth from front to back and allowing you to stitch faster. Stitches worked on a frame are more even than those made when a canvas is hand held. There are several types of frame to choose from and my advice would be to visit your local needlework shop where they will advise you on which type of frame, if any, is most suitable for you. Each person should work in the way that they feel most comfortable, whether it is to work with a frame or to hold the work in the hand. If your method is the latter, the work can be stretched back into shape provided your tension is not too tight.

Needlepoint Stitches

There are many types of stitches used for needlepoint but for the purpose of the designs in this book, where the emphasis is on colour and bold pattern, rather than on textural interest and stitch contrast, only two types of stitches are used – the continental tent stitch and the half-cross stitch. Both are quick and easy and from the front create the same short slanting stitches (see illustrations 2 and 3). It is at the back of the canvas that they differ (see illustration 4). The tent stitch forms longer, slanting stitches, completely covering the canvas and the resulting thickness makes it more suitable for designs to be used for upholstery (footstools, chair seats etc.). Half-cross stitch forms shorter, vertical stitches that do not cover the back of the canvas and it uses less yarn, thus creating a thinner needlepoint than one worked in tent stitch. It is best to keep to one type of stitch to avoid forming ridges on the right side of the work.

2. Continental tent stitch.

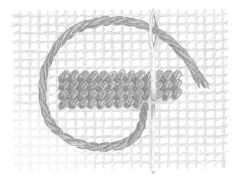

3. Half-cross stitch.

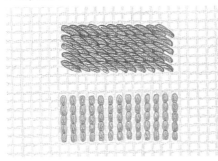

4. Back of the canvas showing the difference between continental tent stitch (above) and half-cross stitch (below).

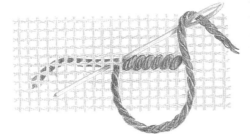

5. To start continental tent stitch.

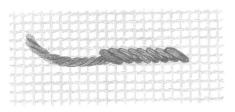

6. The back of continental tent stitch showing the first few stitches worked over yarn to secure end.

For both stitches, cut a length of yarn no longer than 30"/76 cm. Longer lengths are more difficult to work, tending to twist and knot. Additionally, the yarn can wear thin in which case it may no longer cover the canvas adequately. When starting, leave a 1"/2.5 cm-long loose end at the back and work the first few stitches from right to left over it, as shown in illustrations 5 and 6. Work the following row of stitches below the last row and continue to work in rows alternately from right to left, then left to right (see illustrations 2 and 3). For half-cross stitch make short vertical stitches at the back as shown in the illustration, and for tent stitch make long slanting stitches as shown in illustration 6. After the last stitch, darn the end of the yarn through the back of the last stitches worked and cut neatly. If the yarn becomes twisted during work, simply let the wool dangle with the needle hanging down and it will untwist itself.

Tension

When stitching it is important to have an even tension. The term tension means how tightly each stitch is pulled. If your tension is too tight, the canvas may become puckered and the finished needlepoint will be slightly smaller in size. The wool will be stretched and become thin and uneven. If your tension is too loose, loops will form and it will not be neat. Try to keep the tension of each stitch even throughout and the resulting work will be smoother. This will all come with a little practice and is easier if working on a frame.

To Prepare the Canvas

To select the correct size of canvas, refer to the charted design area given with the instructions to each piece. You should add at least 2"/5 cm in addition all round. Before you start to stitch, you need to mark the outline of the needlepoint. Fold the canvas in half in both directions to find the centre. With a waterproof pen, mark the centre lines on the canvas. This divides the design into quarters which makes it easier to count. Now count the threads of the canvas, one for each chart square, to determine the size of the charted design area. Mark the outline. Trace the final outline of the design onto a piece of paper. This is known as a template, and will come into use during stretching.

If you decide to use a frame, now is the time to assemble the canvas on to it. If the needlepoint is to be hand held, it can help to over-stitch or tape the edges of the canvas to prevent them fraying or catching.

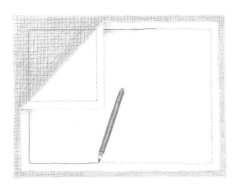

7. How to make a template.

Working from a Chart

All my needlepoints come in chart form and contrary to what many people think, working from a chart is very simple. Each square on the chart represents one stitch. As each stitch is worked over a thread of canvas, you count the threads rather than the holes of the canvas. Each square is coloured in a shade as near as possible to the original wool colour. Sometimes, however, the colours are very similar and to make each one distinguishable from the other the colouring on the chart will be exaggerated for clarity. The colour key provides the exact colour to be used and the photographs should also be referred to.

Where you start to stitch is, I think, a matter of personal preference. I like to work the outline of each motif first and then fill in the centre before completing the background colour. Make sure that the top of the needlepoint corresponds to the top of the chart. If a design is worked in the wrong direction the shapes will be altered, because of the slant of the stitch (see illustrations 8a and b). In this book the top of the chart is always at the top of the page.

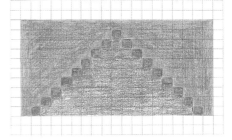

8a. Detail of a chart.

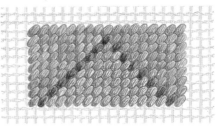

8b. Detail of a worked canvas showing lines created by the slant of the stitches.

Unpicking Stitches

If an area of stitching needs to be undone, due to a mistake, great care must be taken not to damage the canvas. I find it easier to carefully snip each stitch with a pair of small pointed scissors and then to pull out the cut ends using tweezers.

If during unpicking you do cut a canvas thread by mistake, do not panic, it is easy to repair. Cut a small piece of blank canvas from the side of your work and place behind the damaged area, aligning the position of the holes, and the threads. Work the new stitches through both the original canvas and the patch.

Changing the Size of a Design

If you want to increase or decrease the size of design, there are a number of ways you can do this. By changing the mesh size, by repeating some or whole parts of the design or by omitting part of the design.

To change the mesh size, simply divide the number of stitches in the charted design (given on each chart instruction page) by the mesh size. For example: the design for Afghan Patchwork on page 32 is 191 squares wide by 191 squares high. I used 13-mesh canvas which gave me a finished piece of 14.5″/37 cm square. If I had wanted a larger piece of needlepoint I could have used a 10-mesh canvas for a 19″/48 cm square or a 7-mesh canvas for a 27″/68 cm square.

The other methods of increasing or decreasing a design, by omitting or repeating part of a design, are discussed throughout the book, according to the design involved.

Stretching the Canvas

Before a completed needlepoint can be made up it may require stretching first, especially if it has become distorted during stitching and has not been worked on a frame. Do not trim the canvas until stretching has been completed.

To stretch a needlepoint you will need a clean board which must be larger than the canvas and soft enough to take tacks easily; a large set square; a hammer; carpet tacks or drawing pins; and your template.

Place the needlepoint face down and dampen it thoroughly by spraying it with water, or using a damp sponge. Be careful not to soak the needlepoint. Using the template as your guide, nail the needlepoint back into shape. Either begin with a nail at the centre of each side and then work outwards to the corner, or the method which I prefer is to nail one entire side before going onto the next. For both methods it is a good idea to use a set square to check that each corner is at a right angle.

If the canvas is badly distorted steam on the wrong side with either a kettle or a steam iron, being careful not to touch the needlepoint with the iron. Allow the needlepoint to dry completely before removing the tacks, even if it takes several days. If the piece is still distorted, repeat the process.

9. Dampen the back of the work thoroughly before stretching.

10. Nail the needlepoint back into shape. Use a set square to check the corners.

To Join Two Pieces of Needlepoint

The best method for joining two pieces of needlepoint along a straight fold line is to use the decorative half-cross stitch seam. After stretching the finished needlepoint, trim the canvas edge to ½″/1 cm and fold back the canvas along the seam line. This fold should follow the next line of the canvas thread, and not fall across the canvas holes. With the right sides of the needlepoint facing, line up the edges row by row. Using the

11. Joining two pieces of needlepoint.

colour of yarn as specified in the needlepoint instructions, fasten at the back of the canvas and bring the needle through to the front, passing through the first hole at the lower edge of the right hand piece. Now take the needle through the second hole of the adjacent piece to the wrong side and then back through to the front again, passing this time through the second hole on the right hand piece. Continue in this way up the seam, making half-cross stitches. When the seam is complete, fasten off at the back of the work.

Backing a Cushion

Most designs in this book are for cushions. Backing a cushion is a simple process and if you don't have a machine, hand stitching can be equally effective. The material you choose should be reasonably thick, particularly if it is to be a floor cushion. I prefer to use a medium weight Indian cotton, readily available in a wonderful assortment of strong colours. Fine wools and upholstery velvet are also suitable. Take care when choosing the colour of your backing material. It should enhance, not distract from, the design. Zips are optional, but they do allow the cushion pad to be removed easily. Alternatively, you can leave a gap at the bottom of a cushion, stitching it up after the cushion pad has been inserted.

If inserting a zip fastener, you will need to cut two pieces of fabric. To calculate the size, divide the area of the stretched needlepoint in half widthways and add to each piece ⅝″/1.5 cm seam allowance all round. With right sides facing, join at each end of the centre seam, leaving enough seam open in the middle for the length of the zip fastener. Press the seams flat. Pin and tack the zip fastener into position and stitch, using a sewing machine with a zip foot, or by hand using backstitch.

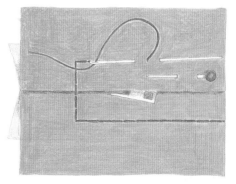

12. Inserting a zip fastener.

If you are not using a zip fastener, you will need to cut one piece of fabric, the area of the needlepoint plus ⅝″/1.5 cm seam allowance all round.

With right sides facing (the zip open if you are using one), pin and tack the needlepoint to the backing. If using cord or piping, read the section on Edgings before going further. Stitch as close as possible to the needlepoint edge using small stitches. Remember to leave a gap just big enough to insert a cushion if no zip fastener is being used. Trim excess canvas and clip the corners diagonally to minimize bulk. Turn cushion cover right side out and insert cushion pad.

13. Stitch the backing fabric to the needlepoint using small backstitches or a sewing machine.

Edgings: Cord and Piping

Both cord and piping, when sewn to the edge of a cushion, make a simple but effective finish.

Always remember when working with cord that it unravels very quickly if the ends are not bound with a small piece of sellotape after cutting. It is best to start along the bottom edge of the needlepoint, either at the end of the gap left for inserting the cushion pad or, if a zip fastener is used, at a $\frac{1}{2}$"/1 cm gap left in the seam when stitching backing to needlepoint. With the cushion cover right side out, push 1"/2.5 cm of cord into the gap and sew into position to secure using double cotton or button thread and a curved needle. Sew cord along right side of seam edge, round back to the starting point. As you sew, be careful not to pull the cord tight. It should lie easily. Push the second end of the cord in next to the first end and stitch this and the gap firmly together.

Piping is made from fabric cut on the bias and wrapped around piping cord. The fabric used can either be the same as the backing fabric or a contrasting fabric. Piping cord is available in a range of thicknesses so you can decide how prominent you want it to be. Cut biased fabric into strips wide enough to wrap round the cord and to add $\frac{1}{2}$"/1 cm on each edge for seam allowances. Join the strips by working a seam along the grain of the fabric. Press the seams. Wrap the binding round the cord, wrong sides facing, and stitch as close to the cord as possible.

Place the cord to the right side of the needlepoint piece, matching the stitching line of the covered piping to the edge of the needlepoint. Place the backing fabric over the piping and pin all three together. To join ends, first join the binding strips with a flat seam along the grain of the fabric. Unravel the two sides of piping cord and trim strands to different lengths. Overlap ends by 1"/2.5 cm. Intertwine to make a smooth join. Stitch in place and trim as for Backing a Cushion, above.

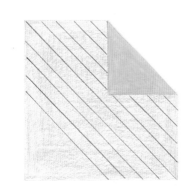

14. Mark out strips along the bias of the piping fabric and cut.

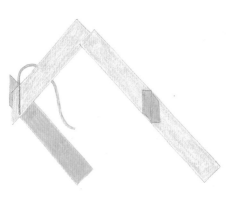

15. Join binding strips. Trim the seam corners.

16. Stitch binding close to cord.

17. Pin piping between backing fabric and needlepoint and stitch together using small backstitches or a sewing machine.

Bolster

The bolster is an elegant addition to a sofa, window seat or chaise longue and very simple to make. Its covers, as seen in this book, are fitted with gathered ends. For the bolster ends you will need to cut two pieces of fabric (see Backing a Cushion for notes on fabric). The length of the fabric will measure the height of the needlepoint (which is the circumference of the cushion pad), and the width will measure the diameter of the circular end. Add 1"/2.5 cm all round for seam allowance. With right sides facing pin and tack fabric to needlepoint along side edges only. Stitch as close to the needlepoint as possible. Fold the bolster cover wrong sides together with long edges matched and work a 'half-cross' long stitch seam (see page 151) across the needlepoint's edges. Turn the cover wrong side out and continue seams across bolster ends, thus making a tube. Press the fabric seams only. Turn tube right side out and turn under a $\frac{5}{8}$"/1.5 cm hem at each end, stitch each hem. At each end of the bolster, using contrast colour thread, hand sew a row of gathering stitches close to the fold. Insert the bolster pad into the tube.

At each end of the cover, pull up the gathering threads to bring the edges of the cover into the cushion. Adjust gathers to distribute them securely and fasten off with a backstitch. I used

18a. Pull up gathering threads at each end of bolster.

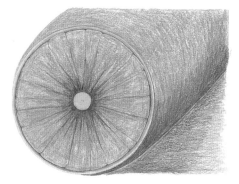

18b. Completed bolster with piping (optional).

button moulds covered in matching fabric to cover the hole left at the centre of each bolster end. In addition to button moulds you could add tassels and trim each end of the bolster with cord or piping (see page 153).

Picture Frame

All you need for completing each of your needlepoint frames, is stiff cardboard and strong masking tape. Make a paper template of your finished and stretched needlepoint. Trace the shape of this template twice onto a piece of cardboard. The first shape with a hole in the centre for the front of the frame and the second

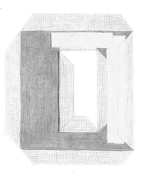

19. Cardboard piece for frame placed over back of needlepoint.

shape without a hole for the back. Trim the excess canvas, leaving a 1"/2.5 cm edge all round. Cut the outer corners diagonally and slit the inner corners as shown in illustration. Position the cardboard piece for the front of the frame over the back of the needlepoint. Fold only one outer side edge of the canvas over the frame and tape securely in place. Leave the three remaining outer edges free. Fold over all the inside edges and tape in place. Position the cardboard piece for the back of the frame over the back of the front piece. Fold the three remaining outer edges over the back of the frame and tape. Slide your picture into position through the open edge.

Rug

The Afghan patchwork rug (page 32) is constructed from separate pieces of needlepoint which are then joined together. Rugs can be made in this way in a variety of shapes and sizes. A large rug made from a single piece of canvas would be heavy and awkward to stitch. Before joining the pieces it is essential that the canvases are absolutely square (see Stretching the Canvas). Each adjoining side must have the same number of stitches so that the square can be joined stitch for stitch. All stitches in a completed rug should run in the same direction. Join each piece by stitching with double button thread. Gently press seams and along side edges fold unworked

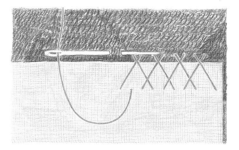

20. Herringbone stitch.

canvas to the back. Herringbone stitch all loose edges of canvas to the wrong side of the rug so that it lies flat (see illustration). Trim excess canvas at corners.

To line the rug I would recommend upholstery hessian as a good backing fabric. Cut the lining to the finished area of the rug plus 1"/2.5 cm seam allowance all around. To stop the lining bagging it should be attached to the back of the carpet with rows of stitches. This is done by working a small stitch through the lining and catching the back of the rug. Bring the needle back up, running the thread under the lining to make the next stitch. I usually work a central line of stitching from top to bottom and then another line from side to side. For larger rugs, further rows of stitching may be required to prevent bagging. Turn under the seam allowances of the lining and slip stitch it to the rug edges.

Cleaning Needlepoint

Needlepoint, when dirty, can either be washed with warm water and a gentle soap powder or dry cleaned. I think it is better to have your needlepoint pieces dry cleaned. Always check before starting whether the yarns you have used have any special washing or dry cleaning instructions and also check your backing fabric to make sure it is colourfast. I use the bath when washing my work so I can lie it flat, right side down. Always be very gentle, never squeeze or rub your needlepoint. Use a large sponge to press up and down on the back, to ease out the dirt. When rinsing change the water frequently. After the final rinse, let the bath or sink empty and use .

a clean, dry sponge to soak up as much excess water as possible. Lie the needlepoint onto a large thick towel and very gently roll it up. This will help to get rid of any further excess water. Finally re-stretch the piece (see page 153).

If a piece of needlepoint has been used to cover a piece of furniture, washing in the bath or dry cleaning is impossible. Vacuum clean thoroughly to remove as much dirt as possible and then sponge with an upholstery detergent, reading the instructions carefully first.

Conversion Chart

Wherever possible the nearest available equivalent colour has been chosen

Appleton	DMC	Anchor	Paterna
105	7242	8594	312
124	7166	9510	483
126	7169	9600	481
145	7205	8420	912
146	7207	8422	911
147	7147	8352	910
152	7692	8896	534
155	7326	8900	533
156	7327	8880	532
183	7413	9384	453
186	7467	9370	432
205	7124	8328	872
225	7196	8400	D211
226	7147	8352	930
241	7361	9306	653
242	7362	9216	652
243	7363	9218	651
252	7362	9196	694
311	7677	9286	751
313	7676	9288	750
333	7361	9306	643
344	7362	9258	652
345	7362	9260	643
354	7424	9096	613
446	7666	8198	841
453	7895	8590	332
454	7895	8592	331
462	7799	8686	544
464	7797	8690	542
474	7725	8060	725
475	7767	8100	723
476	7444	8062	722
481	7399	8806	593
483	4807	8806	592
503	7107	8218	970
504	7127	8204	840
525	7861	8936	522
526	7596	8920	521
554	7784	8098	710
564	7313	8818	504
565	7926	8820	503
566	7650	8822	502
567	7650	8824	501
568	7311	8794	500
584	7529	9648	450
588	7535	9666	459
605	7255	8548	312
626	7439	8164	831

Appleton	DMC	Anchor	Paterna
645	7541	9078	D516
691	7492	9322	645
693	7472	8040	742
694	7504	8042	733
695	7506	8100	732
696	7781	8102	731
714	7226	8508	921
722	7446	8310	871
724	7168	8312	870
726	7303	8312	860
746	7555	8738	502
748	7297	8794	500
761	7724	9324	444
765	7508	9492	D419
766	7508	9520	D411
801	7153	8490	353
802	7157	8490	352
805	7157	8492	350
821	7314	8644	551
822	7797	8690	551
823	7797	8632	550
851	7579	8052	444
852	7299	8744	570
853	7306	8792	501
864	7125	8234	853
866	7920	8238	851
882	Ecru	0386	263
894	7711	8608	332
903	7421	9406	441
922	7594	8736	513
928	7297	8740	510
946	7136	8438	903
947	7138	8440	902
948	7139	8442	901
963	7282	9774	202
964	7273	9776	202
976	7416	9372	451
984	7491	9362	455
994	7360	8164	851
995	7137	8204	941
998	Noir	9800	221

Lengths of different manufactures' skeins and hanks.

	Skein	Hank
Appleton	10 yd/9.2 m	60 yd/55 m
DMC	8.8 yd/8 m	
Anchor	10.8 yd/10 m	
Paterna	8 yd/7.3 m	40 yd/37 m

Index